Draw Me Close

Draw Me Close
A Journey Towards Selfless Faith

Holly Armstrong

Warrior Princess Nation, LLC

Cover design by Soto Visuals

Warrior Publishing, a division of
Warrior Princess Nation, LLC
6935 Aliante Pkwy Ste 104 #423
North Las Vegas, NV 89084
for information email info@warriorprincessnation.com

First Printing, 2024

Table of Contents

What a pilgrimage! You will be blessed by reflecting on this intimate opportunity to see God through the eyes of Holly. I was personally touched by what God can say, do, and reveal to one who loves Him - a supernatural journey.

-Tom Phillips
Senior Advisor, Billy Graham Evangelistic Association

What an amazing story of redemption, sacrificial love, and inspiration! Throughout this book, Holly uses her many personal experiences and trials that God has led her through to capture the hearts of many. While reading the story God has blessed her with, I cried, I laughed, and I smiled so big reading all about the beautiful journeys she embarked on. As a fellow kidney donor, I was surely blessed by the words God gave her, and I know she will be an inspiration to many! I loved every bit of this story, and I am forever desiring to continue to draw closer to God.

-Rebekah R. Nash
Author of "The Greatest Risk of All"

Holly Armstrong teaches, celebrates, and inspires in Draw Me Close. She beautifully tells the triumphs and trials in her life while always pointing all praise and glory to The Father. As a mom of a type one diabetic, I loved reading how the Lord used Holly to bless another in this community.

- Laura Self
Author of "Sweetie: The Story of a Girl Diagnosed with Type One Diabetes"

Dedication

For My Lord and Savior:

Thank You, Lord, for generously showering me with grace, forgiveness, and mercy throughout my life. I never deserved it, but yet You still freely gave. May the following pages only boast of You and your magnificence, and may others notice your incredible, unending love for them as You endlessly seek to draw them near to You. *"I'm thanking you, God, from a full heart, I'm writing the book on your wonders. I'm whistling, laughing, and jumping for joy; I'm singing your song, High God." Psalm 9:1-2 (MSG)*

For Kevin:

Thank you for always agreeing to my crazy plans, no matter how radical they may have been; thanks for trusting God and me enough. Your quiet, strong faith and unconditional love has not only served me all of these years, but also our beautiful children. ILUVU!

For Eliana, Benjamin, and Samuel:

You three are answers to so many prayers. Your faith and dedication to God continually inspires me. Keep shining the Light for the next generation; go and make disciples! I'll love you forever!

For The Rivera Family:

Thank you for sharing Kelley with me and welcoming my family into yours. I love each one of you and pray these words bring you peace and comfort.

A portion of every book sale will go to
Breakthrough T1D (formally JDRF),
in honor of those who suffer
and
National Kidney Donor Organization (NKDO),
in honor of those who sacrifice

Foreword

The Lord brings people across our path along our life journey. Everyone is important, but some stand out with particular joy. Holly Armstrong is one of those young women who came into my life. I will always be grateful that she and Kevin moved from Baltimore at the same time that Tom and I moved to the Carolinas.

Holly has accomplished much in the years we have shared together, but nothing stands out more than her walk, her obedience, her faithfulness to her Savior. Even though there is great age difference, I call Holly a dear, dear friend and example. Creative and innovative, she is the ultimate multi-tasking visionary, able to balance marathon running, homeschooling, homemaking, and serving others as she loves Kevin, Ellie, Ben, and Sam, and most of all, her Heavenly Father, who you will learn has replaced above and beyond the love of her earthly father.

This is Holly's story of joy amid sorrow and challenge. You will see what the Lord can do when God's Word and voice are applied to every step along the journey God gives each one of us.

Who is this Holly? She is God's woman whom He uses daily to inspire hearts to follow Jesus Christ and share Him with others. Her greatest desire is to glorify God while instilling that desire in her children through Bible study, mission trips, and daily encounters. Homeschooling has allowed her to expand the Godly vision of her three very intelligent children.

One of the most humorous but truth-telling stories is one that I remember most every time I drive down Highway 49 in Lake Wylie, South Carolina. Our Community Bible Study (CBS) group met Wednesday morning in a local church on that road across the street from the CVS pharmacy. On another morning, Holly had the three small children in the car heading to the pharmacy, but when she turned left into the pharmacy instead of right into the church, the children exclaimed they wanted to go to CBS, not CVS!

Holly has ensured that the Word is planted deeply into their hearts. This has been displayed as the family travels yearly on missions with funds they have each worked for and saved. There they have become continually involved in the lives of several families and children who have influenced the value of possessions and relationships.

Read Draw Me Close and laugh, cry and be blessed through Holly's story told in her easy, conversational voice. You will be inspired to ask God to draw you closer to Him as well.

Ouida Phillips
Former CBS Teaching Director
Jesus Now Awakening

Introduction

"They triumphed over him by the blood of the Lamb and by the word of their testimony." Revelation 12:11 NIV

"Ok God. I will, if you are positive this is what you want me to do. I will choose to trust and obey. I will move forward and donate my kidney to a complete stranger." - The internal thoughts of Holly Armstrong, circa January, 2020

Friends, I feel the need to set the expectations early on. This book isn't only about my kidney donation process. I have been asked over and over again, "What caused you to donate an organ to a stranger?" For those that don't wish to read on, I'll save you the trouble ... the short answer to that very complicated question is simply "God."

But the long answer is my motivation for writing this book. You see, the short answer doesn't give God the full credit He deserves. In reality, He has been my Trainer and Coach for over four decades, slowly working my muscles of faith, trust, and obedience as He drew me closer and closer to Him. And when He thought I was ready, He finally told me to suit up; He was putting me in the game.

Some time ago, God laid on my heart to write a book. I wasn't sure how to tell my story, so, plain and simple, I procrastinated. In other words, I chose to disobey. The task of organizing my thoughts well enough to give God His credit seemed to continually weigh me down. I'll be honest and vulnerable; the thought of writing an entire book felt too astronomical of a task for me to tackle. It was like having a massive mess in my garage, so large that I just didn't know where to start. I knew I needed to do something about it. But the task seemed so formidable that I simply kept putting it off. I'm guessing that I'm not the only one who has ever procrastinated tackling a task because they simply didn't know where to start!

But as an educator, I had to take my own advice. When first assigning ten-page term papers to my students, I would see the apprehension in their eyes. But after teaching them the beauty of an outline, and an easy-to-follow, step-by-step process, they were able to see the assignment as manageable. How do you write a term paper or an entire book? The same way you eat an elephant - one bite at a time. God spoke to my heart and said, **"Just start the outline already. Remember your objective. Give me glory and encourage others, and the pages will practically write themselves."** Fortunately, I finally chose to obey. And the pages wrote themselves.

So, how do I answer the long, complicated question of why I donated my kidney? The first step is really asking the correct question. It's not really "why" I donated an organ. The real question to ask - and what this book attempts to answer – is, "How did God build in me a faith muscle so great that I was willing to do such an unconventional thing?" In His immeasurable grace and patience with me, He did it one faith-building testimony at a time.

Each chapter in this book is a story; some long and complicated, some simply short and sweet. But each one is an account of where God worked on my faith. My principal Trainer knew that some days had to be "leg days" while others were "cardio." But in the end, my entire body would be strong and ready.

Again, I'll be honest. (Because no one wants to read a dishonest testimony!) Over the years, there were times when I was compliant and obedient, but there were also moments when I stomped my feet like a three-year-old having a tantrum and screamed to God with my arms crossed and a pouty lip. "No! I won't. I don't want to!" And I didn't. And sometimes, after the tantrum, I would cry and eventually cave. But each success and failure prepared me for when that BIG ASK - literally giving a piece of myself away - was requested.

My family and I play a silly game in the car where we yell, "Punch Buggy" whenever we pass a Volkswagen Beetle. We have a whole Armstrong family set of rules.

If it's a convertible, you get two punches. If the convertible top is down, you get three, and so forth. This game has trained our eyes to notice the Beetles all over the road. In the same way, God has spent years training my eyes to notice Him, His beauty in ordinary things, and His precepts in everyday living. Once you see Him, you can't unsee His mighty signature on everything.

The following pages are my journey of faith. In between each chapter are miniature devotions I wrote along the way. A dear friend of mine once said, "I love seeing God through your eyes." I pray that as you read along, you, too, are able to see God as I have seen Him. You can learn to train your eyes to notice all of the faith-building experiences that God is performing in your life, and ultimately, may you also pray, "Draw Me Close."

Grab your favorite mug of coffee or tea, have a seat, and allow me to converse with you a bit. Fair warning though, once you have seen God, I promise it's hard to unsee His handiwork in both my life and hopefully in yours...

Preseason Conditioning:
Learning to Trust

1

Draw Me Close

"Draw near to God, and he will draw near to you"
James 4:8 (ESV)

I grew up in the church. In fact, I have technically been baptized three times. I know that is not conventional or necessary, but it's my story. As an infant, my parents had me sprinkled at a Lutheran church. They separated by the time I was in kindergarten, and I grew up not knowing my father. My mother sought comfort in God and the church. So, when I was eight years old, we attended a small Baptist church; it was there that I first heard the call to walk down the aisle and be saved. God was beginning to draw me to Him. Though I did not fully understand it, I was baptized later that day by complete immersion.

Life was hard for my mother, who was raising my older brother and me. She battled depression, heartache, financial strains, working multiple jobs to make ends meet, extra extended family drama, taking my father to court for child support, and so forth. I believe she did the best she was capable of. For some seasons, we would attend church multiple times a week; in others, we could go months before attending again.

However, I was given a "We Sing Bible Songs" cassette tape in elementary school. I listened to those songs repeatedly on my

Walkman or Boombox. Then, as I grew older, I would listen to contemporary Christian favorites like Amy Grant, Michael W. Smith, Steven Curtis Chapman, and Sandy Patty. Their songs hid Truth in my heart, even when I was not attending church and listening to sermons or Sunday school lessons. When my teen years hit, my mother was busy working and attending nursing school, so we went to church even more sporadically. I also started dating a guy in high school who was not a churchgoer. He and his crowd of friends slowly drew me away from my immature faith.

But in the end, no one is to blame but me. I made stupid choices in high school, even though I knew better. I knew that I was blatantly choosing to sin against God. But as a girl growing up without a father, I craved the affection my boyfriend gave me, even when it turned abusive in many ways. It was still attention, but I felt trapped without an escape.

However, I still succeeded academically. Living on the impoverished east side of Baltimore, I knew the only way out was through an education. I had many dedicated teachers who invested in me and encouraged me to seek a higher education. I graduated top of my class.

Even in the middle of my most sinful years, God still showed me favor. There remained a tiny part of me that inwardly knew He was the reason I was succeeding. So, when asked to give a Commencement speech at my graduation, I chose to go against the grain and began my speech in the public school setting with a prayer thanking God. But I inwardly felt like such a hypocrite.

Three days after graduation, when I was merely 17 years old, my mother moved three thousand miles away to live with her new husband in California. She had just met him a few months before and felt her parenting job was complete. So, she moved on with her life, leaving me feeling utterly rejected by another parent.

At my current stage of life, I finally understand some of the emotions she must have been experiencing. I recently launched my oldest to college, and my two sons are only a few short years away from leaving home. For the last 19 years, I have dedicated my life and career to homeschooling, and I wonder what I will do for myself once my kids no longer need me. But I still have a husband. My mother was feeling the emotional crunch of the impending empty nest during my senior year of high school. She had dedicated her life to keeping food on the table while bettering her own education to provide us with a more stable life. But as my older brother graduated, and I became busy with sports, a boyfriend, and extracurricular activities, she must have felt very lonely and in need of a change.

She found her second husband on the internet....in 1997 using dial-up internet. They met for the first time in person during Christmas of my senior year. Then, in March, she flew to California and eloped with him. She returned to Maryland for my last two months of high school, and then, seeing her job as a single parent complete, she moved across the country to begin the next phase of her life.

This turn of events left me entirely alone—except for that boyfriend. I let his decisions and desires dictate my life, relinquishing full control of my heart and body to him. The fear of being completely alone disabled me from making wise choices.

Even though I had been baptized twice at this point in my life, I had never truly made the decision to follow Christ, to allow Him to lead my heart, mind, and soul. That would not come for a few more painful years of feeling lost......

To be honest, I really do not want to write about this time in my life. It was the blackest, darkest moments. I felt so utterly hopeless that I tried downing bottles of Tylenol multiple times to take the pain away. But my boyfriend's fist would usually stop me midway. He, too, was lost and utterly afraid of being alone. Put two emotionally distraught and volatile lost souls like that together;

violence and heartache are bound to ensue.

By God's grace and protection, it never occurred to me to research more effective suicide methods.

I often hear people say stupid stuff when they read the news. They will stumble upon a domestic violence article and say aloud things like, "I can't see why she stays with that kind of man." Or, "Why doesn't she just leave his sorry @ss?"

I understand all too well. The fear of the unknown is often greater than the known. The fear of utter loneliness is more paralyzing than being with someone who occasionally shows acts of love.

The moral of my last few paragraphs is - please do not say stupid stuff. You can never understand until you have walked in someone's shoes. If you have nothing nice to say, it's best to say nothing at all.

So, I stayed with that boyfriend through my first year of college. That year, I made way too many foolish decisions—so many that I no longer recognized myself.

I was on an academic scholarship to a state university, to which I commuted. High school had been easy for me. College, however, was incredibly hard. I'm unsure if I wasn't well prepared academically or if my tumultuous life outside of college was merely defeating me. I had registered for college, wanting to earn a Biology major. AP Biology was easy during my senior year of high school, and I had an uncle who died of AIDS when I was in middle school, so I had grand plans of becoming a researcher who found the cure to that nasty disease.

During my freshman fall semester, I enrolled in Chemistry. My high school AP classes were small, with 5-10 students, and provided loads of personal attention. My college Chemistry class, however, was in a lecture hall with hundreds of other ill-prepared, emotionally drained first-year students. I received my first "C" ever in my life in that class. I was devastated but also relieved at the same time. That class taught me about the beautiful Bell-Shaped Curve, which magically transformed my 52% grade into a "C" on my transcript, bringing me much emotional relief. Nonetheless, with an academic scholarship to maintain, fear crept in. I could not fathom taking multiple more Chemistry classes to earn the Biology degree.

So, I switched majors. Geography and Environmental Systems sounded fun. I enjoyed learning about my state capitals in elementary school and preferred environmental biology over microbiology. In all honesty, I did not know much about the major or future career options, but I enjoyed my Physical Geography class and figured I could get better grades in Geography classes.

During the spring semester, I even began working in the Cartography lab, which was in the basement of the Social Sciences building on campus. Fellow Geographers referred to it as the "Dungeon" since the small Geography program was primarily based in this one dark hallway of classrooms and computer labs. I was still dating that high school boyfriend at the time, but I was starting to feel a tad better about life. The nerd in me was relieved to be succeeding academically once again, but the emotional and physical abuse was still an ongoing issue in my private life.

One day, though, I became fed up with the literal darkness. I was working for the Cartography professor, building a map of a state park, and I looked around the room. It was so dark and claustrophobic in this tiny dungeon of an office. There were tiny basement windows at the top of the concrete walls where I sat alone, but I wasn't tall enough to reach the curtains to open them. I so desperately needed just a little light to shine in my life.

Exasperated, I marched down the hall into the other Geography computer lab, where a bunch of upper-class students worked, and I boldly spoke up, "Could the tallest boy in this room come open some curtains for me?" I don't remember batting my eyes or being flirtatious at all about this, but something about my request must have been endearing. A 6'3" senior stood up, looked around the room as if sizing himself up against the competition, and came to my rescue.

That statement has so much meaning. He certainly came to my rescue that day. In fact, that tall Geography major named Kevin Armstrong would come to rescue that first-year damsel in distress that day and for years to come.

Kevin.... there is so much to say about him, and I promise you will learn much more about him if you continue to read this memoir. But for now, know that he is a light giver. He literally came and opened those curtains for me that spring day while nonchalantly flashing me that handsome smile of his. He was tall, dark, and handsome, just like I had prayed and daydreamed about in those tween phases every young girl goes through as they begin to envision their future.

Kevin was a senior and a hockey player. He initially seemed like a preppy kind of guy, and I had heard that he had graduated from a private Catholic high school. He often wore a shirt and tie.... to college!?! (At the time, I did not realize that the hockey team dressed up for game days. I just thought this guy was THAT preppy. And I knew that no girl from the "ghetto" had a chance with an older, sophisticated guy like that.)

But that day, he was unknowingly used by God to shed the first glimmers of light into my heart and soul. The curtains were finally slowly opening. We barely saw each other again that spring semester, and I didn't think much more about him.

The summer between my first and second years of college, I hit the lowest I had ever felt. My boyfriend and I were not only still fighting, but we were also young and naive and even decided to work together that summer. I was with him constantly. We were both lifeguards at a small apartment pool. We would get up, work out, be lifeguards all day, and make stupid choices at night. Rinse and repeat; it was a terrible season of life.

The choices I made that summer left me feeling dirty, low, out of control, and even darker than before. My attempts at downing that Tylenol bottle were unsuccessful as well. Only that boyfriend knew the extent of my distress. He was all I had, abusive or not. I did have my little, lazy beagle, Mindy, my sweet little guardian angel, who continued to love me without judgment and needed me to make it home each night. She was my emotional support animal before such terminology even existed, a true gift and companion for me during that troubling season of life.

By God's grace and sovereignty, I somehow lived to see my second year of college. That fall, when I walked into the Geography lab, I ran into that tall, helpful boy, Kevin. In fact, I was utterly surprised to see him. I asked, "Weren't you a senior last year?"

He grinned and said, "I'm a senior again." He had not failed any classes but had merely spent more time playing hockey his first year of college than taking enough credits to graduate on time. I like to see it as God using his hockey and my poor ability to do Chemistry to merge two souls who needed each other.

Kevin spent his summer in California as an intern at Sequoia National Park. His summer was amazing and starkly different from the one I had just experienced. He and I would often talk about California together. Although I had yet to visit Sequoia, I had often visited my mother and stepfather since her move there. In addition, I had an aunt living in the Bay Area. I also enjoyed hearing about his joy-filled experiences over the summer, for they helped drown out my tormenting memories.

During one of our conversations, it was made known that he had a girlfriend, and I reluctantly remained with that same boyfriend from high school. But there was something drawing Kevin and me closer together. His attention made me feel loved, special, and seen, not dirty and abused like my boyfriend had always left me feeling. Time with him was different and pure, and I wanted more of it. I also learned that he was not in a happy relationship himself.

One thing about me that is still true to this day is that I am always cold. One evening, Kevin and I were both in the Geography lab. He was proctoring and knew I would be there to work on my school assignment. Thoughtfully, he had brought along an extra sweatshirt in case I grew cold.

The fact that he noticed a need of mine and took the initiative to serve me was something completely foreign and captured my aching heart. Long story short, we kissed that night for the first time, and the trajectory of my life forever changed. It's not the best of stories to be kissing another boy who had a girlfriend while I was in the third year of my own relationship. It's certainly not something either of us is particularly proud of. But God can even use our poor choices to accomplish His will.

Kevin and I decided that same night we wanted to start a relationship together and, thus, would both break up with our significant others that week. So, we did. We broke hearts. He felt guilty. I felt guilty. But I also felt free for the first time in forever, free to make my own choices, free to follow what made me happy, and free to really love and be loved.

The two of us became inseparable. I learned what it was to be treated with respect, to have a gentleman open the door for me, to never lay a forceful hand on me, to gently caress and not merely use my body. Yes, we were in love, but we were definitely not followers of Jesus. Yet!

Kevin graduated that second senior year. I graduated the following year, cashing in all those AP credits to finish college in three years. I found myself at another May graduation. This one was not full of fear and anxiety like high school had been, but one of hope and excitement. Kevin proposed, and I, of course, said, "YES!!!" I was deeply in love with this strong, stoic man, and I had grown to enjoy being truly loved. Light was beginning to shine in my life once again.

A few days after college graduation, I began working at the same company as Kevin. He was mapping crime, and his connection helped land me a job as a Computer Trainer, where I would teach law enforcement personnel Microsoft Office products. I instantly adored my job, for it utilized my people skills and my natural affinity towards helping others. The family joke to this day is that the only thing I was ever able to really locate with a Geography degree was a husband, but I soon learned that my calling was in education.

The company we worked for was an agency funded by a grant given to the University of Maryland. This meant I was technically a university employee and thus entitled to free graduate-level courses. Kevin and I bought a house together in August, were married in October 2001, and in January, I began earning my Master's in Education at night and online while working full-time as a trainer during the daytime. Those first two years of marriage were beautifully busy. Thankfully, we commuted and ate lunch together daily; otherwise, it would have been hard with my evenings full of studying and Kevin's spare time building his own side business to help make ends meet. God was keeping our marriage strong even when we had yet to invite Him into it. God is pretty awesome like that. He sees your potential before you even realize it yourself. He lays foundations before you ever grasp what He is building.

Life was good. We both had well-paying jobs. I was furthering my education. He was starting his own side business. We were homeowners living near Kevin's family, whom we loved and visited often. We had even begun taking his sweet, widowed grandmother, Meemaw, to church on Sundays. I spent time with Meemaw every Wednesday night; she taught me to crochet, and I felt the love of a wise woman. She was the first to truly welcome me into the Armstrong family, and I think she was secretly also praying for me. I never told her all about my past hardships and feelings, but she was no fool. She could perceive that I had many deep wounds in need of healing. I thought I was helping her all those evenings battle loneliness when in reality, she was another Armstrong moving back curtains to allow more light into my life.

While driving onto campus the last semester of graduate school, a song came to my head. I had not heard it in years, but I could not get the dang thing to leave my brain. I was in a happy mental space, quite content being a married woman to a perfect gentleman and raising our three beagles. (Mindy was no longer lonely either, for she was given two furry, mischievous brothers over the years). But something still felt like it was missing. I could not put my finger on it, so God decided to enlighten me.

That bright, bright, sunny, crispy autumn day in 2003, while looking for a parking spot on campus, the song "Draw Me Close" began to blare in my brain. Michael W. Smith recorded that song, and I grew up listening to it on cassette tape. Since meeting Kevin, all I listened to was country music. He really wasn't that preppy Catholic boy that I initially thought him to be. Instead, he was a pickup-driving, country music-loving, good ol' boy, but he did not listen to Christian music. I, myself, hadn't listened to it in a decade or more. But this song…. every single word of the verse and chorus came flooding back to me in an instant.

Draw me close to You
Never let me go
I lay it all down again
To hear You say that I'm Your friend

You are my desire
No one else will do
'Cause nothing else can take Your place
To feel the warmth of Your embrace
Help me find the way; bring me back to You

You're all I want
You're all I've ever needed
You're all I want
Help me know You are near

Without realizing it, this song wasn't just on repeat in my head for days, but it became my first actual prayer to God in a very, very long time. Light was shining in, and my heart could do nothing but respond. I had tried for over a decade to make it on my own, with a boyfriend, with an education, with employment, and with a husband. But "No one else would do" and "Nothing else could take HIS place" in my life. My prayer soon became, "Help me find a way to bring me back to You."

James 4:8 (ESV) declares, *"Draw near to God, and He will draw near to you..."* And that's what I began to do. God kept up his promise, for He always does.

Soon after this pivotal day, when I first heard God asking me to draw Him close, and when I first began speaking to Him again, a beautiful opportunity arose. Kevin and I had been escorting Meemaw to church on Sundays. It was an elderly congregation where us two young adults felt as if we were the nursery of the church, but it brought Meemaw joy to attend with her. One Sunday, Kevin made plans to golf with some buddies, and I offered to drive Meemaw alone to church, but she hadn't planned to attend that particular week due to another obligation she scheduled.

This left me with some choices, and life is sometimes about making the right choices at the right time. I could skip church that weekend, attend Meemaw's church alone, or impulsively try a new church. The thought of going unaccompanied to a church full of older men didn't appeal to me, nor did sitting home alone sound enjoyable to my extroverted self. So, I found myself walking through the doors of a large church, sitting quietly in the back.

I don't remember the songs we sang or which sermon was

preached, but I remember feeling the presence of God so strongly, along with an intense feeling of repentance for attempting to live life without Him. I felt God drawing close to me, reminding me that I had not only been singing to Him but that he had been singing to me. As I had prayed for Him to "Draw me close," He had been singing to me, **"You're all I want."**

Here, I realized that I had a Father who wanted me. After being abandoned by my own biological father during my formative years, I struggled with the abstract thought that a Heavenly Father loved me and desired a relationship with me. God was singing to my heart that day, standing there with wide open arms, calling out for me to walk towards Him. He needed me to truly accept his Son's sacrifice on my behalf so I was worthy enough to run into his presence. And I did.

"At that moment the curtain of the temple was torn in two from top to bottom. The earth shook, the rocks split and the tombs broke open. The bodies of many holy people who had died were raised to life." Matthew 27:51-52 (NIV)

Light flooded into my life, amazing me with its brightness. Love enveloped me like I had never truly encountered, always craved and sought in the wrong places, but never truly experienced. I was forgiven. I was accepted. I was redeemed. I was loved. I was held. I was whole. I was learning to trust. The fruit of obedience would take time and maturity, but the first signs of trust were finally blooming in my soul.

Points to Ponder

1. How has God used someone or something to shine a light into your darkness?

2. Do you know someone who needs you to shine a light into their darkness? If so, what can you do or say to them this week?

3. Has God ever used music to teach you His Truths?

4. Have you noticed God drawing you closer to Him lately? If so, how?

5. Take some time today to talk to God. Feel free to ask Him to "Draw Me Close." Write down ways that you feel Him speaking to you.

Devotion: You Never Lose Your Value

Facebook, June 2021

"I got up out of bed, grabbed a dollar bill, and started taking pictures of it.

It was crumpled and then put in the trash. It got stepped all over. Then, it was grabbed, taken outside in the rain, left in the mud, and then pushed deeper into the mud.

It then received another setback, with its corner being ripped. But then it was taken back inside to safety, gently wiped off, corner mended, and laid out to dry before going back in my wallet...
    For it is STILL a dollar....

And never once, no matter what it had been put through by others, NEVER once lost its WORTH!!!

I don't know who needs to hear this today, but my heart is heavy in prayer for you. You might feel like you are in the process of being stomped all over right now by the people around you. Or you may have been removed from your safety and kicked out into the elements. You may be dealing with health problems and injuries, or maybe you are recovering and drying out but not quite ready to be with others. Or, maybe when you look in the mirror, you wonder why you don't look like you used to before "whatever" happened.

Whatever it is, you are worthy. Let me repeat myself: no matter what it is, no matter what you have been through, you are worthy! Do not give up hope; better yet, know your worth in God's eyes!!

"Look at the birds. They don't plant or harvest or store food in barns, for your heavenly Father feeds them. And aren't you far more valuable to him than they are?" Matthew 6:26 (NLT)

2

Growth

"Then Jesus said to his disciples, "If any of you wants to be my follower, you must give up your own way, take up your cross, and follow me. If you try to hang on to your life, you will lose it. But if you give up your life for my sake, you will save it."
Matthew 16:24-25 (NLT)

The trajectory of my life changed the day I made the pivotal choice to ask Jesus to reign over my life. It would also change the trajectory of others. I no longer wanted to live for myself but to do all I could to live for Jesus. I was married to a wonderful man but an unbeliever. Sure, we were attending a Methodist church with his grandmother, and yes, he graduated from a Catholic high school, but none of that meant that Kevin truly wanted to live for Christ.

Unfortunately, the American church experience often sets people up for failure. Many grow up thinking they are Christians because they believe the Christmas and Easter stories told. However, to truly follow Christ, one must fully grasp the significance of Christ and his sacrifice, repentance, and forgiveness. In Matthew 16, Jesus told his disciples that it would take full devotion to be one of his followers.

I wanted all in. I was ready, or so I thought. But I was also now unequally yoked and not mature enough in my faith or emotionally brave enough to tell Kevin all about my experience. I did the only thing I knew to do: I prayed.

I started a covert operation. Secretly, I switched our morning alarm clock radio station from country to Christian music. I was honest enough with Kevin, telling him that I had tried a new church and suggesting that we try it together. *"You know, since Meemaw's church is so old. She has plenty of friends there and won't miss us."* I began journaling, too. I may have lacked the courage to speak to my husband about my new faith, but I didn't neglect pouring out my heart and prayers to God each evening.

I finished my Master's degree that December and started a new job as a training consultant. I also finished hiding my truth from Kevin. I became bolder in my requests. The new church that had led me to Christ also had a young adult ministry that met in a pastor's home once a week. I mustered up the courage to suggest we try it. *"You know, for a community of friends our age."* And then, the church offered a faith and science class that piqued the interest of my deeply logical husband.

He went along with all my requests, and somewhere along the way, Kevin fell in love with Jesus, too. We grew quickly close to God but so much closer to each other now that we had invited God into our marriage for the first time. The first nine months of 2004 were such an explosive year of spiritual growth for Kevin and me. We couldn't get enough of church. We attended Sunday School and community groups and played volleyball with some of the pastors at church multiple times a week. We studied books of the Bible and memorized Scripture. We surrounded ourselves with a community built on faith and fellowship.

This was also the time when we attempted to begin a family of our own. I was consumed with the desire to become a mother. Many of our new friends at church were young parents, and having grown up in a broken home, I craved a family of my own more than a dying man in the desert craves water. I felt that I needed to get pregnant. Were we financially ready? No, not in the slightest. Was I growing too old and worried about my fertility window closing? Nope, not at all, for I was still in my early 20s. I had this insatiable need to be part of a family who loved Jesus. I wanted to have children and raise them to be followers of Jesus. The only problem was that I wasn't getting pregnant right away.

Anyone who has ever counted days, checked basal body temperatures, and felt the heartbreaking defeat of month after month of no conception can relate. When you have the instinct to procreate but can't, the emotions play nasty tricks with your mind.

In my immature faith stage, I felt for sure the whole thing was my fault. I had let my ex-boyfriend abuse my body. And I was determined that God was punishing me for that. And worse, he was punishing my husband as well.

Thankfully, the wonderful faith-filled community we had built around us prayed with and for us. They patiently taught us Truth. I slowly learned the characteristics of a loving Heavenly Father who wants to bless his children rather than punish them. The love and prayers of our friends would prove utterly necessary as September 2004 rolled around.

Points to Ponder

1. Are you currently engaged in a faith-filled community that can uplift you during hard times? If not, what's stopping you?

2. Do you still harbor unnecessary shame and guilt for sins God has already forgiven? If so, ask the Holy Spirit to allow you to feel the full freedom of God's forgiveness.

3. Is there anything holding you back from fully sharing your faith with others?

Devotion: Follow Closely
Facebook, circa 2019

"Thought to ponder for my fellow 'Christ followers'...

I was thinking about this today as I was driving behind Kevin to drop off his car to have some work done.

I had zero clue where the shop was, where we were headed, and how long it would take to get there.

I had never been there.

All I knew was that I was to follow Him.

To get to the same destination, I had to stay close, turn when he turned, brake when he braked, etc.

It hit me that to follow Christ, we must also do the same.

Follow.

Follow closely.

Mimic the one you are following.

Otherwise, you will just get lost.

And if you ever do get lost, just call Him and He will help you get back on track.
That's all. Just wanted to share that today."

"My sheep listen to my voice; I know them, and they follow me."
John 10:27 (NLT)

3

Intense Loss

"Even when I walk through the darkest valley, I will not be afraid, for you are close beside me. Your rod and your staff protect and comfort me." Psalm 23:4 (NLT)

Sheila was my best friend. A few years younger than me, she was a fierce, 4 foot 11, 90-pound Puerto Rican with the largest smile and an infectious laugh. She had been the receptionist at the organization where Kevin and I worked. We instantly bonded, for being young females in a law enforcement, male-dominated work environment wasn't easy.

Sheila married young, right out of high school, and became pregnant a year later. Kevin and I were asked to be the baby boy's godparents. We were absolutely honored and rushed to the hospital when John Damien was born. We attempted to spoil that precious little boy every chance we had.

Unfortunately, Sheila and her husband soon divorced, leaving her a very young single parent. My heart broke for all her struggles, for I had grown up witnessing first-hand the hardships single moms face.

Sheila found it necessary to temporarily move to Puerto Rico to live with family, but then she returned to the Maryland area to be local for all the divorce and custody court hearings. Unbeknownst to me at the time, she had secretly moved in with a new boyfriend.

When Sheila returned, we often had her and Damien over. (She called her baby by his middle name and even had it tattooed on her ankle.) Sheila began attending church with us in the summer of 2004, attending young adult ministry picnics and letting Kevin and me babysit whenever she needed a break. We even began planning to move her closer to us so we could help with the baby more.

I called her one Sunday in early September to ask about attending a picnic when a man answered her phone. It was early in the morning, and I recall joking with her, asking why a man was answering her phone that early, knowing full well that it must have meant he had spent the night. All she told me was his name (I'll simply refer to him as "R"), and she promised to tell me more later. We chatted for a few short minutes and agreed to see each other later that week. I never had the privilege of hearing her voice again.

Tuesday morning, the day after Labor Day, I was ecstatic. I had recently discovered that we were finally pregnant. We decided to hold onto that secret for a few weeks, but in the back of my mind, I couldn't wait to tell my best friend. At this point, Kevin and I still commuted together, but I worked as a training consultant for a startup company a few miles from his office. That morning, I remember sitting at my desk for a few minutes, reading through email, when my phone rang. A mutual friend and coworker of Kevin's called me devastated. He asked if I had heard about Sheila. I said I had just spoken to her the morning before, but not today. This friend read to me a Washington Post article about a young lady who had been stabbed to death in her home the night before. He told me it was our dear, sweet friend, but my brain couldn't fathom the horrific truth. So, he forwarded the article to me. I remember staring at my computer screen in utter shock, reading the gruesome details that confirmed Sheila's fate. Her full name. Her address. The fact that it all happened as her two-year-old son was in his pack-and-play in the very same room. The facts stabbed through my initial disbelief and penetrated my soul, leaving it bleeding in agony.

I frantically left. I don't remember all that happened in the next few hours or even days. All I remember is the gut-wrenching shock and brokenheartedness that my dearest friend was gone forever. I would never tell her I was pregnant. I would never hear her laugh again. She would never cuddle her son again.

Oh, Damien. My sweet, sweet little buddy. How was he to grow up without the doting love of his mama? I couldn't handle it all.

As pieces of the puzzle came together, we slowly learned the facts. "R" had been abusive to Sheila. She felt ashamed to be living with him but couldn't afford an apartment of her own. That is why I had only days before learned of his existence; her shame must have kept her silent. This also explained her incredible excitement to move closer to us. She had secretly been trying to free herself from his evil grip, all without me even knowing.

Sheila's last day of life began with trying to bring Damien to church. "R" roughed her up in their apartment parking lot. Neighbors witnessed and heard her screams for help, and the police were called. "R" was taken downtown to the precinct. Sheila was petrified, even getting a restraining order against "R" and having the apartment complex change the locks that very day.

However, the court-ordered piece of paper and new locks did nothing to save Sheila's life. "R," in a fit of rage, immediately upon his release from jail, used lawn furniture to bust into the apartment through the back sliding glass door. He stabbed Shelia so many times it was immeasurable. He thrust his weapon so deep into her abdomen it penetrated the mattress beneath her. The details were overwhelming to learn.

Mourning my friend was one of the absolute hardest things I would ever have to do. I knew she loved Jesus. I knew she would be pain-free in Heaven. I had the promise of seeing her again. But it still hurt like crazy. We buried Sheila on Saturday, September 11, 2004. I didn't think I could ever hurt more deeply. But, the next day, on September 12th, I miscarried my baby.

I had planted some daisy seeds in a pot as part of a women's ministry event during the time I knew I was pregnant, at the end of August sometime. It was an activity that was designed to teach us to wait on the Lord. I was so excited thinking that those daisy seeds would blossom, possibly at the same time in May when I would birth my first child. It was too early in the pregnancy, so I never had an ultrasound to reveal the gender. But my soul knew it was a baby girl. She will forever have the name Daisy May in my heart.

When I lost that precious baby, who was but merely the size of a seed in my body, I didn't know what to do. God did, though. He knew that Kevin and I would suffer such heart-wrenching pain. To miscarry our first baby and to tragically lose a precious friend were both terrible, but it felt completely unbearable for them to happen the same week.

I had to trust God, though. I didn't know how I could or what that would look like, but I knew it was necessary. Thankfully, Kevin did, too. And by the grace of God, we were already established in a faith-filled community where close friends would lift us up in prayer and be there for us.

Those who think they can follow Christ without community are listening to the lies of the enemy. It is within those faith-filled communities where growth happens and lives are changed. For me, that autumn was where hope was found.

Knowing that I needed to heal emotionally was no surprise, though I wasn't sure how. To be honest, I had never really dug out the father or ex-boyfriend wounds yet, and to add these traumas to my fragile emotional state felt overwhelming. As much as I loved commuting with Kevin every day and getting paid great money to be a training consultant, I knew something needed to drastically change. Our church was hiring an administrative assistant to help the youth and young adult pastors. It was a significant pay cut for me. I wouldn't be using my Master's Degree in Instructional Design. I wouldn't eat lunch daily with my husband anymore. I didn't even know how we would pay our bills.

I didn't care, though. I merely knew I needed more of Jesus to fill the holes in my heart, and the thought of taking my lunch break to talk to Jesus in the sanctuary was one step in my healing process. Every day, I simply took my pain to Jesus. He heard me cry and held me in my darkest moments. It helped, too, to be surrounded by a work environment of pastors who were all very sympathetic to my emotional status and would often lift me up in prayer during my weakest, most vulnerable moments.

God always shows His love. When His children hurt, He does, too. He never leaves us alone with our pain. Instead, He carries us through it.

My other healing came from sweet Damien, who was now living with his 21-year-old father, who was suddenly thrust into single parenthood upon Sheila's death. Damien had lost his mama. I had lost my baby. I saw a solution here. I would have adopted that sweet boy in a heartbeat, but I knew he had a father who loved him, plus Sheila's sisters and mother would have jumped at the guardianship before me.

But Damien's father allowed Damien to spend weekends with us. We created a bedroom for him in our home and bought clothes and toys for him. This arrangement enabled Damien's father to have frequent breaks, and he allowed us to have a child to love and hold. Slowly, Damien's father acclimated to parenthood, and the weekends with Damien slowly got further and further apart, and we were healing from our hurts. God was providing for everyone while also preparing us for the next phase of life.

Points to Ponder

1. What are your reflections on the quote, "When His children hurt, He does, too." Does it bring you comfort to know that you are not alone in your pain?

2. When traumatic experiences happen to you, do you find yourself running to or away from God?

3. Looking back, how do you see God caring for you and your deepest wounds?

Devotion: Be Thankful for The Tools in Your Toolbox
Facebook, circa 2020

"Something has been on my mind lately, and I hope I can finally express it well enough to post it. Life gives everyone very different trials and tribulations (and 2020 has been full of them!!!) But with each trial, we are also GIVEN 'tools' to get through that trial.

For instance, have you ever had something break in your home, and you needed to run to Lowes to buy a new tool just to fix it?

Or ever get crutches because of an injury? And then later, a friend needs to borrow that tool or those crutches? You are ONLY able to assist them because you first went through your trial.

On a more emotional level, have you ever gone through a loss or hard time and then learned to handle that circumstance?

For instance, in 2004, when I had my miscarriage and my best friend was murdered, I relied on other friends who had suffered as I had because - unless you have been through something like that, you can't fully understand. And since 2004, I have then been able to comfort those who later lost close loved ones - because I have made it to the other side of that emotional journey myself.

Sometimes, we get angry or frustrated with the trials that give us these new 'tools.' But when you are going through a trial, who do you turn to - the friends who have the 'tools' to borrow or the friends who have never dealt with that issue before?

I guess I just want to ENCOURAGE everyone going through any trial right now. God is simply growing your 'toolbox!'

Lean on GOD and the friends He places in your life.

And then be willing to share those 'tools' when others begin their trial.

Those 'tools' really are GIFTS even though they don't seem like it in the moment they are given.

1 Peter 4:10-11 (CEV) says, "Each of you has been blessed with one of God's many wonderful gifts to be used in the service of others. So use your gift well... Everything should be done in a way that will bring honor to God..."

Points to Ponder...

-What gifts/tools do you have that could be used to help others?

-And are you using them?

-Are you walking around with a grateful heart that you have them, or are you resentful that you had to get them?

"Summing it all up, friends, I'd say you'll do best by filling your minds and meditating on things true, noble, reputable, authentic, compelling, gracious—the best, not the worst; the beautiful, not the ugly; things to praise, not things to curse. Put into practice what you learned from me, what you heard and saw and realized. Do that, and GOD, who makes everything WORK TOGETHER, will work you into his most excellent harmonies." Philippians 4:8-9 (MSG)

4

Answered Prayer

"Children are a gift from the Lord; they are a reward from him." Psalm 127:3 (NLT)

By January of 2005, about fourteen months since I first recognized God singing me my heart song and three short months since Sheila's death and my miscarriage, Kevin and I were both standing in our church baptismal, declaring that we wanted to make Jesus Lord over our lives, marriage, and future family. (Yes, this would end up being my third time being baptized, but it was the first time that I undoubtedly understood what it meant and truly chose it for myself. And for the record, it would be Kevin's first and only baptism.)

At this point, we didn't know if we would be blessed with any more pregnancies. As God drew us closer to Him, He would slowly reveal His plans. While helping chaperone a youth retreat that winter, the speaker challenged us. He asked the young adult leaders to be examples for the teenagers. He said, *"I want you to hold out your hands, palms raised. What is it that you are tightly holding onto? Are you trying to control something? Open your hands. Give it to God. Have you been hurt and holding onto your pain? Give it to God. Trust Him. Just lift your hands and release your pain, your worries, and your anxieties to God. Surrender to Him."*

At that moment, I held out my open hands and chose in that instant to give God complete control. I desperately wanted to make Kevin a father. I longed so deeply to become a mother. But I had to first trust God. I had to acknowledge that He was the giver of life. I can't create it on my own, no matter how much I want it. Only He could. I chose to submit to His plan and trust Him with our future. The act of physically holding out my hands in front of everyone became my personal sign of submission and my ever-increasing faith put into action.

I learned that day that trust is a choice. You can follow closely if you trust the one ahead of you. You can go to the unknown if you believe the one you follow knows the way. I chose to trust God with whatever He found best for our family. I knew surrendering meant giving up MY plans for my life and trusting God for HIS, no matter how pain-filled or joyous the future might be. I will admit that it was slightly scary to relinquish control and extremely exhilarating all at the same time.

In that conference center, surrounded by thousands of teenagers and leaders, and with my eyes tightly closed and hands held high, I submitted. Later, I would find out that Kevin did, too. God spoke to us both about the same heart issue. Tears streamed down my face, and I felt joy for the first time in months. *Psalm 126:5 (NLT)* came to my mind, *"Those who plant in tears will harvest with shouts of joy."* Months prior, Kevin had read this verse to me as I lay in the fetal position on our bed, sobbing over the loss of Sheila and our baby. God brought it to the forefront of my mind. It was harvesting time; I had doubted that joy would come again, but here it was.

I realized that I didn't need a baby to feel God's joy; I simply needed to understand more about His ways. He is enough. He is also a promise keeper, and His plans are always perfect. God wants

His children to willingly follow Him. He is the Good Shepherd, and He alone deserves the reins. Too much toil, conflict, and pain occur when we constantly try to control things ourselves. The desire for control sucks the joy right out of one's soul and separates them from their Creator. That day in January of 2005, I finally realized the error of my ways and accepted God's plan, whatever it may be, for Kevin and me.

Miraculously, immediately after that act of submission, we became pregnant. God also gifted me with the name Eliana Faith only weeks after learning of the pregnancy. Eliana means "Answered Prayer." I had never heard it before, and at the time, we hadn't even known the gender yet. But God revealed to me that our baby was going to be an answered prayer to not only Kevin and me but to many throughout her lifetime. Because God had named her, I felt confident of her future. He would hold the reins for our lives and for hers, too. I was able to fully rely on Him to care for us and our growing child.

Looking back, I'm so thankful for the God-ordained timing of our lives. He truly knew what was best. In God's magnificent timing and plan, He had already set us up for success. Working at our church during my pregnancy proved easier than had I still been consulting. As my belly grew, I was able to slowly drop down to part-time hours and eventually stop right before delivery. In His provision, God also taught us how to budget on a lower income, training us to be prepared to live on just one income. A year prior, we weren't financially, emotionally, or spiritually ready to become parents, but God knew that and was patient with us. Making us wait seemed so hard at the time, but it was worth it.

In late October 2005, we were blessed with holding our baby girl in our arms. Ellie, as we affectionately would call her, was a precious, beautiful baby. Her delivery was quick and intense and almost ended with an emergency C-section, but God answered our prayers. Ellie had to spend her first few days in the NICU due to a potential heart murmur and jaundice, but God again answered our prayers, and she came home a healthy infant. The joy of the Lord was in her, and it was evident to all who met her. She smiled often, and anyone who met her claimed she was the happiest baby they had met. In addition, even early on, we knew she was spiritually blessed with the gift of "language." She spoke full sentences months before most toddlers. Today, she continues in her giftedness as a Spanish major in college, who effortlessly became fluent in that second language and desires to learn more as well.

When she was just a few months old, we gathered our pastor, friends, and family into our home, and we dedicated her back to God. Just as Hannah had after receiving the baby for which she prayed, we promised God to raise our child to be His servant. When she was only a year old, I began taking Ellie to the local nursing homes and assisted living centers to spread God's joy to others. At 6, Ellie heard about a local missionary who needed funds and asked if she could sell some items to raise money for her. We agreed, and in her blog about fundraising, she wrote:

"A 6-year-old answered my prayers. This beautiful little girl of the Most High King has moved me to tears and been the most sincere example of unselfish generosity that I have encountered in these crazy, awesome, unbelievable months of fundraising...Little Ellie came up to me with a little tin of money she personally had saved for my trip. She smiled shyly, and I listened in awe as she told me where the money came from. As the afternoon unfolded, her mom filled me in further. Led completely by the Holy Spirit, Ellie did an incredible thing. It started with her allowance. When before, she would save her allowance, usually for a toy or treat, she was now putting ALL her allowance aside for me. She had been saving for months to buy an American Girl doll. She donated this money to me... But further still, God was working in this little girl's heart. She wanted to give more. With her parent's help and guidance, she

started selling her toys. Her beloved doll house. Her brand-new birthday presents, and many others. And putting all the money in the little tin to give to me. Although the number itself doesn't matter, I just want to share it because it shows how much this little girl can teach us all to give of our bounty. All in all, there was $237 in the little tin. And she is six years old. I can actually truthfully say that this little girl has given me more than the vast majority of the adult donors who are supporting me. I appreciate each dollar and each donor with every fiber of my being, but you have to agree that this is one special story and one unique child of God. How many of us would be willing to give God every single spare dollar of our income AND all the money we have been saving for that new car AND every gift we receive, AND sell our most beloved possessions to allow money to be used for His purposes? Her name is Eliana. I think God has a really soft, poignant side that He chose to answer those anxious prayers from months ago through a truly remarkable little girl whose name means 'answered prayer.'"

Ellie wrote in her 6-year-old journal about the day she blessed this missionary with the funds....

"I felt happy about giving her the money. I want her to go to all the countries she has to, to tell everyone about Jesus. I would like to go with her if I was old enough. I would want to tell everyone about Jesus because I want everyone to know about Jesus."

Ellie was raised to rely completely on God and began sharing that truth at a very young age. Now, in college, she continues to be an answer to prayer for us and others. Her love of sharing the gospel of Jesus with everyone is still a blessed calling on her life.

Trusting God's ways wasn't always easy in the moment, but it proved to be best in the long run. Learning to relinquish my tight grip and trusting God with everything would become the central truth that carried me through more challenging times the future held.

Points to Ponder

1. Is there anything in your life which you are holding tightly and trying to control? Consider releasing it to God and experiencing freedom in submission.

2. Have you ever thought about the meaning of your name?

3. Have you experienced God's answer of "No" or "Not yet" to your prayer requests in the past? Looking back, do you see God's provision in those circumstances?

Devotion: Walk By Faith, Not By Sight

Facebook, January 2021

"The kids enjoyed their devotion today.

I taught them *2 Corinthians 5:7 (ESV), "For we walk by faith, not by sight."*

I blindfolded them and had them follow my voice as I repeated the memory verse.

They had a ball. I had them zigzag. And then I'd ask them if they knew where they were.

They didn't.

But then I asked them if they were comfortable with that and they said, 'Yes.'

I told them it was because they trusted me. (We had learned about trusting Jesus yesterday.)

I told them that in life they might not always know where Jesus is sending them, but they were to trust Him and simply follow His voice."

5

Go To The Land I Will Show You

"The Lord had said to Abram, 'Leave your native country, your relatives, and your father's family, and go to the land that I will show you.'" Genesis 12:1 (NLT)

Becoming a stay-at-home mother was the best. I absolutely loved it and never regretted giving up my career to be a mom. God had blessed us with the baby for whom we had desperately prayed, and I was incredibly thankful. Unfortunately, our mortgage and bills weren't as happy. Kevin suggested we take Dave Ramsey's Financial Peace Class at a local church when Ellie was about nine months old. Upon learning Biblical principles of money management for the first time in our lives, we knew we had to pray about some very important decisions.

We started budgeting, tithing, and paying off debt, but we still felt like we were slowly sinking into a financial abyss. That's when we felt the need to investigate moving away from Maryland, where we had both grown up and where we had Kevin's family close by for Sunday dinners and free babysitting. After much prayer, research, and number crunching, we felt confident that God was moving us to the Carolinas. Real estate prices were cheaper there, and Kevin could find work in his field. We would still be close enough to drive back on vacations to visit family.

In early 2007, we sold our home. Kevin and I felt strongly that we were to radically tithe off the sale price of our first home. It wasn't conventional, but our faith had grown strong over the last few years, and we trusted God knew what was best. We had learned through our finance class and through experience that holding tightly to money wasn't Biblical.

Trusting God with our money and moving south took trust and obedience.

One thing 2007 taught me, though, was that spiritual attacks are bound to happen when you submit that much to God.

Before we were able to leave Maryland, we suffered numerous hardships. My grandmother passed away. My mother in California was quite ill in the hospital for many weeks with a staph infection, and we traveled with Ellie to visit her. In addition, some last minute, very expensive mold was found in our home that needed repairing before we could sell it.

But we continued following God's direction.

Leaving Maryland, our friends, family, jobs, church, and everything that we knew was an incredible act of faith for us. If you have ever moved to a new state, you know how scary, frustrating, and exciting it can be. Navigating new areas, visiting new churches, finding new doctors, and making new sets of friends can all be overwhelming.

We landed temporarily in a rental home in a suburb of Charlotte, North Carolina. Kevin found a job working for a local police agency as a crime analyst. He wasn't fond of the job, but it was a means to an end. He sacrificed so much for his family during those first few months. Ellie and I tried to settle in, but I was incredibly homesick and lonely. I was also incredibly nauseous, for we soon discovered that I was pregnant again.

In the early years of our marriage, we kept a journal — just a spiral notebook in which we wrote to each other. This excerpt from October 5, 2006, shows how we trusted God and each other in preparing to move our family....

I wrote to Kevin, *"We've been really busy these last three months - ever since we decided to move, life has been hectic. Thank you for being the calm in this storm! You truly are my better half! Thank you also for all the countless hours you've spent away from Ellie and me renovating the house to sell. It was a sacrifice for you, I know, but you never complained. You are wonderful, and I look forward to starting on this new journey with you by my side. Wherever we end up, all will be alright because we'll be together. It's exciting and scary at the same time. I'm thankful God is in the center of our marriage, for He'll guide us and keep us close to Him and each other when times get tough. Thank you for being you and loving Ellie and I so very much!"*

And he responded, *"Hello Princess. Thank you for being such a great wife and mother the last three months. It has been hectic, and sometimes it seems we don't have time to appreciate each other. I know we will be happy wherever we end up. Funny how the location keeps changing! God will provide for us so let's just enjoy the ride. ILUVU"*

Points to Ponder

1. How is trusting God with your money an act of trust and obedience?

2. Have you ever deeply thought about how you are managing your finances and if they align with principles taught in the Bible? If not, what could you do today to begin learning more?

3. Is there a direction in which God is trying to send you? How are you responding to His call - would you be willing to move your family if God directed you to do so? If not, what would be standing in your way?

Devotion: Hear, Trust, Obey
Facebook, June 2023

"Yesterday, God woke me up at 5:38 am. He told me to go to the YMCA. (I normally go at 5 am on Wednesdays and Fridays for the early class - but today, He told me to go on a Thursday).

God distinctly told me to go—not to work out but to meet with an older gentleman who was in some of my classes and who went every single day. For this devotion, we will call him "Bob." Bob works out often and has been going through a lot of life struggles. I tried arguing with God that I had to get ready for VBS, and I must have been mishearing Him.

Of course, God spoke to me again - patiently - and said, *"Go to the Y and talk to Bob."*

So, I got up and immediately dressed for VBS, not workout clothes. I arrived just before 6:00 am when the 5am class was letting out. I saw Bob walk out.

He said, "Hey Holly! What are you doing here?" (Because I was obviously not dressed to work out.)

I said, "I was waiting for you, Bob." Then we went upstairs and walked the track for 45 minutes while chatting.

I told him, "God woke me up to come to talk to you. So how are you, and what is it that's going on for God to not let me sleep in today? lol"

He started pouring out his heart about feeling lonely after his 45-year marriage ended in divorce, how he didn't know how to grocery shop since his wife had always done it, how he had been through a *lot* of physical illnesses lately, and mostly how he just felt that God wasn't listening to his prayers.

I was able to reply with, "But Bob... God IS listening. Hence, He asked me to come chat with you: to remind you that He hears, that you are never alone, and that you need to be in Christian fellowship - a church, Bible study, men's group, etc. - to remind you that you are loved."

He got teary-eyed and said that I reminded him so much of his late mother. He said that she loved Jesus very much.

I asked him, "What would your mom be suggesting to you during this season of trials, if she were still alive? Would she be reminding you that you are loved by others and by God? Would she be reminding you to return to church? Would she be reminding you that you are never alone?"

He could only nod his head.

He then looked up at me with a huge smile on his face.

I could literally SEE the difference it made for him to hear the Word of God spoken into his life that morning. Joy and hope had returned.

I was smiling a big smile, too.

I share this story with you as a reminder - we don't always listen and obey God, but when we do, people's lives are changed, including ours. We need to be deep in prayer and LISTENING to God so that we can follow through with His requests of us. His purpose will always prevail. Had I not obeyed, God could have sent someone else to talk with Bob that day, but since I obeyed, I was able to physically see hope restored in the face of a hurting child of God. Bob and I were both blessed.

6

Not Today, Satan!

"Be prepared. You're up against far more than you can handle on your own. Take all the help you can get, every weapon God has issued, so that when it's all over but the shouting you'll still be on your feet. Truth, righteousness, peace, faith, and salvation are more than words. Learn how to apply them. You'll need them throughout your life. God's Word is an indispensable weapon. In the same way, prayer is essential in this ongoing warfare. Pray hard and long. Pray for your brothers and sisters. Keep your eyes open. Keep each other's spirits up so that no one falls behind or drops out." Ephesians 6:13-18 (MSG)

During Ellie's pregnancy, I had a few complications and scary moments that had me panicking I could lose her. One day early in this new pregnancy in 2007, after only being in the Carolinas for about 4 to 5 weeks, I felt that intense panic rise again. Kevin was at work, and I was home alone with Ellie. I knew enough to give my anxieties to God and rebuke Satan for trying to distract me. So, I got down on my knees during Ellie's naptime and prayed fervently for our growing family. I shook my fist at the devil and declared, *"There is nothing you can do that will harm this baby. I'm trusting him/her to God. Amen."*

By this time, Ellie was awake, and I needed some fresh air. I told my sweet toddler that we were going to walk the dogs. She begged me to "walk, walk, walk" instead of being strapped into the stroller, but an inner instinct assertively told me to strap her in that day. I wasn't sure if I just needed a faster pace or if God was warning me of something. The latter would prove to be true.

With Ellie strapped into the stroller and our dogs leashed, I closed the door behind me and crossed the street to begin navigating through our new, quiet rental community. I had only walked a few houses away when I glanced up and saw an enraged pit bull escape from a house further up the street. It was running right at us, gnarling at my two beagles. Having grown up in Baltimore, I always carried pepper spray and quickly pulled it out of the stroller.

The pit bull initially only had eyes for my dogs. It barreled towards us, and instantly, a massive dogfight erupted in front of me. I pushed Ellie's stroller to the side and attempted to pepper spray the muscular aggressor that was trying to maul my two sweet beagles. The spray did nothing to stop the attack besides leave me coughing. Instinctively, I reached my arm into the fight and tried to pull the angry beast off my fur babies. Instead of breaking up the fight, I was now a victim of it.

The pit bull chomped down hard on my left arm and viciously dragged me to the ground like a K9 officer taking down a criminal. I began screaming for my life. Everything happened so quickly.

The dogs barking and my shrieks alerted a neighbor who came to my rescue. I later learned that this neighbor had decided to take off work that particular day to build a fence in his backyard. He normally would not have been home then, nor armed with a 2x4 in his hands. He bravely ran over to the commotion and literally beat the pit bull for it to release its grip on my now shredded and fractured arm. But God had divinely placed him in the right place at the right time to provide for me in my moment of need.

As the neighbor chased the dog away, I crawled over to the stroller to verify that Ellie was unharmed and to grab my cell phone. Kevin says it was the worst call he has ever received. I was frantically yelling something about a dog attack, blood, seeing the bone, and crying for him to come home immediately. He later would tell me that he prayed and sped the whole way home, not knowing who was injured or to what extent.

God saved my babies that day. There is no doubt. Had I not listened to that still, small voice to put Ellie in the stroller, what happened to my arm could have easily killed my toddler. Had my neighbor not been home and armed, the attack could have been more severe, and my pregnancy affected. But not today, Satan!

Afterward, in the ambulance, I remember begging the EMT to pray for my baby, and that kind lady did just that. I wish I could find her to thank her for that very important prayer. It calmed me down and distracted me from the pain. Due to my pregnancy, she couldn't administer any pain medications, but that's not what I craved in those moments. I simply wanted my unborn baby cared for in the best way possible...through prayer!

I was released from the emergency room that night, and Kevin's parents had been contacted, and immediately started driving south to assist us. With my arm in a cast, I was unable to lift Ellie in and out of her crib. This meant I would need help. Kevin had just started his new job and couldn't afford time off. Kevin's parents stayed for a week. My aunt, who was like a third grandmother to Ellie, then arrived for two weeks of assistance. And my mother came in the fourth week. God used that incident to help me with my homesickness. Take that, Satan! *"You intended to harm me, but God intended it all for good. He brought me to this position so I could save the lives of many people." Genesis 50:20 (NLT)*

We were blessed with family that first month. This was so helpful during my first trimester in a new city and recovering from an intense injury. So many happy, precious memories were made with our family in town during that season. We visited the local botanical gardens and parks, and Ellie grew closer to her three sets of grandparents.

In case you are wondering, the pit bull was put down that evening. Thankfully, it tested negative for rabies, and my growing baby was miraculously unharmed in the incident. And my beagles walked away with only minor puncture wounds.

For the record, to this day, pit bulls are still Kevin's and my absolute favorite breed of dog. Just like humans, they can be trained for evil or for good. I never, ever want the telling of this story to sound as if the breed was dangerous. No, it was the gang members, who were also renting in our neighborhood, who had trained that particular animal to viciously attack; they were the danger.

While we were renting, we began the process of building a house just over the border from Charlotte into South Carolina. By July of that same year, the house was completed. At six months pregnant, we moved yet again. My first Carolina summer was spent pregnant, and wow was it much warmer down here than in Maryland! Ellie and I spent our days meeting new neighbors at the community pool, but Kevin was still very unhappy at his job. We began praying for his situation, and in October, he was hired to work his dream job for a mapping software company. This shift brought him much joy and great benefits, but also a bit of travel.

I was due in November with our baby boy. As we did with Ellie, we wanted to give our children meaningful names. So, we decided to name our firstborn son Benjamin Michael, meaning "Son of the South." He was to be a beautiful blessing to us for our act of trust and obedience in following God's lead to move to South Carolina. Michael was not only in honor of my late uncle, but we also desired this baby to grow up to be a mighty messenger of God's love to others.

Ben's birth story is one we are asked to tell often. It is a doozy.

We lived about 30 minutes south of the hospital. Kevin had just returned the day before from work travel. This is the first of the amazing blessings. The fact that he was in town for Ben's dramatic arrival is one for which I'm especially thankful.

I called Kevin at his office, which was 45 minutes away, and asked him to come home early, for I wasn't feeling well. We had planned for Ellie to stay with our new Sunday School teachers whenever we went into labor, and we had asked neighbors to take care of our dogs for us. We had only been in the new home for a few months, and Kevin had only just begun his new job three weeks prior. Everything was still so new, but God perfectly provided for us.

When Kevin returned from work, we decided to begin driving Ellie to our friends, who would keep her overnight for us. We strapped her in the backseat and began driving. As we were pulling out of the neighborhood, I called the dog sitter and gave them a heads-up in case we stayed to deliver Baby Ben.

We weren't even 5 minutes up the road when my water broke. This in itself is not an emergency, for with Ellie's delivery, my water broke at home, and we safely made it to the hospital with time to spare. November 14, 2007, however, would prove to be a unique day of trials and miracles.

When my water broke, I felt the baby instantly drop. We were about 20 minutes away from the hospital and decided that we needed to head straight there. Calling our friends, we asked them to meet us there to pick up Ellie instead of dropping her off with them. We didn't think we would have the time for the extra stop.

Then, the baby crowned. I frantically screamed at Kevin to drive faster. I was breathing through the quickly advancing contractions while holding onto the Assist Grip handle above the car window. (In Baltimore, we always had a more vulgar name for these handles, but to write this story as cleanly as possible, Google tells me that car engineers officially call them Assist Grips.)

So, with my hand clutching these handles, my mouth screaming for my frazzled husband to drive faster, and with my daughter wailing in the backseat out of fear since Mama was in such intense pain, the three of us zipped and zoomed through 5 pm traffic to the hospital. The main road we were traveling on had two lanes going in each direction and a long middle lane that was used for turning into all the various businesses along it. Kevin repeatedly used that middle lane to pass anyone who wasn't also going 25 miles per hour over the speed limit that evening.

I remember praying as we ran red lights, drove onto curbs to maneuver around stopped cars, and repeatedly used the middle lane to pass on the left all the confused and angry drivers we hurtled past. I prayed for Jesus to protect us and all the other drivers. I also prayed for my husband to drive even faster. I will admit that these prayers were quite audible.

About 3-4 miles away from the hospital, we were almost there, and the baby felt ready to slide out of me. I begged Kevin to pull over and, *"Just catch the baby!"*

He decided it was best if he just drove faster, so he did. He swerved, ran another red light, and used that middle lane to pass another car.

But then…. BOOM! Unbeknownst to us, that middle lane ended, and a concrete median began. We hit it, going about 45-50 miles per hour. We busted both tires on the driver's side, and the car tipped onto the two passenger-side wheels. By God's grace and protection, we did not flip or roll. But the car's safety features were so shocked at our new 45-degree angle of motion that my passenger side airbags exploded into my face.

Then, plop. The car tilted back down on two rims on the driver's side and two wheels on the passenger side.

Kevin and I both turned around to make sure our two-year-old was safe. Of course, she was startled and shrieking even louder, but thankfully, she was unharmed. Miraculously, we all were safe.

There was still one impending problem: the baby was still coming! I resoundingly reminded Kevin of this and pleaded with him to catch the baby.

I'll pause the retelling of this dramatic tale for just a second. Kevin and I often share this story with people when they learn that Ben wasn't born in a hospital. And, I think Kevin ruthlessly, yet humorously, enjoys telling new dads this story as a fair warning when their wives approach their due dates. But at this point in my version of the story, I always interject a joke. It wouldn't be the same if I didn't share it here as well....

In all honesty, men only have two real jobs in bringing a new life into this world. One, they need to impregnate the wife. And two, they need to drive her to the hospital when it is her time to deliver. Sure, they may rub some feet or go on some late-night weird food acquisition adventures, but the task of growing a new life falls on the mother, for it occurs within her body. It is the mother who deals with the scrunched bladder, the stretch marks, the contractions, soreness, etc. The father merely stands alert, ready for his main role in taxiing the laboring wife to the hospital.

Just as my body kicked into its instincts of feeding and protecting the growing baby and rearranging organs to make room for this beautiful new creation that November evening, Kevin's instincts also kicked in. He was laser-focused and determined to do his darndest to get me to the hospital in time.

So, with a few short miles to go but with only two rims and two wheels, a crying toddler, and a frantic wife in mid-delivery, my poor husband did all that he knew to do. He drove. Bumpety, bumpety, bumpety down the road, we slowly went, scraping metal to asphalt, inching our way toward the hospital.

My body, however, screamed that we weren't going to make it there in time, so I naturally howled at my husband to call 911. He picked up his cell phone and had almost dialed the three most memorized numbers when I desperately pleaded to the only One who could really help me, *"Dear God, I need an ambulance!!"*

You can't make this story up. Believe me, if I had been writing a fiction account, I wouldn't have made my character scream so much, and I surely wouldn't have recorded how many road laws my husband broke that panicky evening. But this story is true, and believe it or not, what I'm about to share is an absolute miracle and 100% fact.

As soon as I called out to my Heavenly Father, and before Kevin could finish dialing 911, an ambulance instantly turned onto our road and drove right towards us. I noticed it, pointed, and screeched, *"AMBULANCE!!!!!"*

Kevin dropped the cell phone mid-dial, turned our mangled car onto the oncoming traffic, and flagged that angelic vehicle down.

The paramedics ran out, one trying to calm my frazzled husband down and the other racing over to my side of the car.

Later, I learned that the person who spoke to my husband told him, *"Sir, take care of your toddler; we have your wife."*

They brought around a stretcher and rolled me onto it, quickly placing me in the ambulance. Instantly, they were stripping me of my maternity pants and learning that, no, I was not overreacting; the baby was literally crowning and primed for delivery.

Three pushes - head, shoulders, body - and I met my beautiful Benjamin for the first time. However, between pushes 1 and 2, the divinely placed paramedic ordered me to pause the pushes. The umbilical cord was tightly wrapped around my infant's neck and, unbeknownst to us, strangling him. Had I delivered him on the side of the road into Kevin's untrained hands, the act of delivery may have killed my baby. But no, God had big plans for this child. He had already survived a brutal dog attack in utero. He was now the survivor of a car accident and near strangling, and he had only but taken his very first breaths of oxygen.

All this happened at an intersection in rush hour, one block from the hospital. The ambulance stopped where Kevin had cut it off, and the paramedics rushed to catch, detangle, and wrap my precious infant. He was safe and delivered into my arms, where I cried tears of relief and big breaths of release, the kind of breath after the danger has passed and you can finally inhale deeply again.

As soon as Baby Ben was in my arms, I asked the paramedics to open the ambulance doors so I could introduce Kevin to his firstborn son.

To my utter shock and surprise, there was no mangled car, no husband, and no toddler still next to the ambulance. I remember crying out, *"What?!?! He left?!?!"*

Remember how I told you we were right around the corner from the hospital at this point and how the paramedics had ordered Kevin to take care of his toddler and that they would take care of me? Well, Kevin thought that meant they were going to use the ambulance's four working wheels to speed me the rest of the way to the delivery department at the hospital. He knew he needed a head start with only two rims and two wheels, so he scraped metal to asphalt all the way to the hospital while the paramedics unwrapped Ben's umbilical cord from his tiny neck.

This story is amazing, funny, scary, spiritual, and so much more. And believe it or not, our fun that day wasn't even over.

Poor Kevin scraped metal all the way into the hospital parking garage, unbuckled Ellie, and sprinted into the maternity ward, where he frantically asked to see me, his very pregnant wife who had just been rushed by ambulance to the delivery room. The medical staff had no record of me or even that an ambulance was called out to a car accident involving a delivery. There simply had been no time to initially radio in the call when Ben's life needed immediate saving.

Thankfully, Kevin's confusion and panic only lasted a few

moments because we soon arrived at the hospital, and our new family of four was together for the first time.

Years later, we would humorously learn that the fire department was dispatched to the hospital because smoke could be seen coming out of the parking garage. All that metal to asphalt left a few people bewildered that day. Some were even afraid that the hospital was on fire when it was really an extremely tired Ford Focus wagon exhaling from its own traumatic evening.

After painfully delivering the placenta in the hospital and enduring excruciating stitches to repair a massive private tear that I suffered during the expeditious delivery, I was able to relax and hold my baby again.

If we hadn't already experienced enough stress that day, Kevin received a phone call a few minutes later from our dog sitter, asking if he could return home to let her in. Apparently, the key I gave her didn't work, and my pregnant brain never thought to check the duplicate after it was made. Kevin, of course, couldn't drive back home, for the smoking car was being towed away for its own much-needed rest and recovery. Thankfully, we were able to reach our next-door neighbor, who managed to find one miraculously unlocked window on our second floor where he could climb into our home and then unlock the front door for the sitter. That last hiccup was the icing on the cake of one of the most memorable evenings of our lives.

As humorous as it is to retell it 17 years later, I'm also still in utter awe of God's provision. Serious injuries to any of my family members could have happened that night. We could have accidentally caused a serious wreck on numerous occasions; my baby could have died of asphyxiation, and so much more. Thankfully, God placed the right people in our path at just the moment He knew we would need them. I was so relieved to find out that they were NOT on the way to another call at that moment, for I would have felt terrible for stealing someone else's ambulance in their time of need. God knew all these details. He miraculously answered my prayers that night and for the last nine months of praying over the safety of that child. No weapon formed against me shall prosper! Not today, Satan!

When moments like these happen, I can do nothing but humbly pray, "*Thank you,*" and promise to never doubt, always trust, and obey. I will continually tell this story to my children and anyone willing to listen. It is part of our testimony, and I pray it draws you closer to the Writer and Provider in this story.

In case you aren't already aware or simply need reminding, God loves to do immeasurably more for his children. Ten years later, I enrolled my kids in a summer camp, where we would have the amazing opportunity to be reunited with the dear paramedic who delivered Ben. Five years after that, God allowed us to meet the second paramedic from that ambulance. We love getting together with these new friends and retelling our sides of this crazy birth story.

Today, my Benjamin Michael has lived up to his name in both stature and faith, being a strong messenger of Christ's love to all he meets. Every few years, on his birthday, we drive him up to the intersection where he was born and snap a picture with our growing son. We want him to fully understand how much God loves him and has a mighty plan for his life, preserving it in miraculous ways well before his very first breath. This truth that God intervened on his behalf is one we pray he continues to grasp throughout his lifetime.

Jesus had a crazy birth story, too. Most are familiar with it from Christmastime. At the last minute, Mary and Joseph had to travel to Bethlehem on a donkey, which I'm sure was way bumpier than driving with two rims on a paved road. And God would provide every single detail then, too - a safe delivery, visitors to witness the miracles, and a hope for the future for all humanity. As much as my Ben loves God and is a light to those he encounters, he pales in comparison to the brightness Jesus brought into this world. If you have never read it, I challenge you to pick up your Bible and turn to Luke chapter 2 and/or sit quietly and marvel at the lyrics of the Christmas song, "O Holy Night."

Oh, holy night! The stars are brightly shining
It is the night of the dear Savior's birth
Long lay the world in sin and error, pining
Till He appeared and the soul felt its worth
A thrill of hope the weary world rejoices
For yonder breaks a new and glorious morn
Fall on your knees! Oh, hear the angel voices
Oh, night divine
Oh, night when Christ was born

I can't help but fall on my knees when I think about the provision of God, not only to me on that November evening but 2,000 years ago when he not only provided for my salvation but that of all mankind. Not today, and not ever, Satan!

Points to Ponder

1. Do you remember to call on God in your deepest times of need? Is He the first person you call on when you need help?

2. Can you look back and see a time when God miraculously provided for you in your dire time of need?

3. Have you paused to consider how miraculous Jesus' birth was and how eternity-altering it was that God humbly came down to us while we were yet sinners?

Devotion: The Most Wonderful of Stories

From the Jesus Storybook Bible, written by Sally Lloyd-Jones, and read to the Armstrong children many, many times....

"Some people think that the Bible is a book of rules, telling you what you should and shouldn't do.

The Bible certainly does have some rules in it.
They show you how life works best.

But the Bible isn't mainly about you and what you should be doing.

It's about God and what He has done.

Other people think the Bible is a book of heroes, showing you people you should copy.

The Bible does have some heroes in it, but...most of the people in the Bible aren't heroes at all.

They make some big mistakes (sometimes on purpose), they get afraid and run away.

At times, they are downright mean.

No, the Bible isn't a book of rules or a book of heroes.
It's an adventure story about a young Hero who comes from a far country to win back his lost treasure.

It's a love story about a brave Prince who leaves his palace, his throne-everything-to rescue the ones he loves.
It's like the most wonderful of fairy tales that has come true in real life."

7

Full Circle

"Those who plant in tears will harvest with shouts of joy."
Psalm 126:5 (NLT)

Ellie and Ben were born just 24 months and two weeks apart. Life was good for the most part. Ben suffered from a serious respiratory infection when he was only one month old. He was hospitalized, needing a spinal tap to his tiny little body, and the event was scary, but God provided healing. Kevin traveled often for his new job but was always a present father who offered me whatever support the kids or I needed. And, whenever possible, he invited us to travel with him. If he was within a few hours' driving distance, we would tag along and explore new zoos, aquariums, beaches, museums, and parks while he worked, and then we would have family time in the evenings.

Something felt missing, though. I was incredibly blessed with a loving husband who was growing in his faith, two healthy children - a boy and a girl - a home, a growing community of friends in my Community Bible Study, my neighborhood, and a new church. What else could be missing?

I didn't want to seem ungrateful to God, but my motherly instincts suggested that our family was not yet complete. So, a few week after Ben's first birthday, we began trying to have one last child. Unlike our first time, which took many, many months to conceive to only end in heartache, we were blessed with a quick pregnancy this last round. Since we already had one of each gender, and whole sets of wardrobes to accommodate each, we decided to wait until delivery to be surprised with this last baby. The gender didn't matter, for he/she would simply be the cherry on top of our family, the last final touch to really complete its beauty.

I was due in September of 2009 and had a new obstetrician due to insurance changes. When I first went to him early in the pregnancy and told him about Ben's delivery, he highly suggested we schedule an induction to ensure I safely delivered in a hospital this time. As the pregnancy was nearing completion, I asked my doctor if we could induce on 09/09/09 since nine had been my volleyball and softball number growing up, and having a birthday of all nines just seemed cool. The doctor informed me that he was off on the 9th and suggested the next available date, 09/11/09. There was no way I would willingly give my child a September 11th birthday. After working outside of D.C. on that fateful Tuesday in U.S. history and witnessing the smoke of the Pentagon from my office window, I couldn't fathom that being a choice. I wasn't going to pick a day of infamy for my blessed child's birth. If God wanted my baby to have that birthday, He would have to induce me Himself. At last, we agreed upon an induction date, and the doctor scheduled me for Saturday, September 12th.

Kevin's parents traveled south to watch Ellie and Ben for us, and Kevin drove me to the hospital. There, my water was broken, and I walked 2-3 laps around the maternity ward and immediately went into labor. For those reading this who suffered hours and hours for each delivery, bless you. My body apparently becomes impatient when labor begins and practically spits my babies out. We chose a natural birth with no pain medication, but some things that hurt the most have the highest value. God showed me undeserved favor with those quick deliveries.

On September 12, 2009, just before noon, my doctor exclaimed, *"It's a boy!!"* and my Samuel David breathed his first
breaths. This sweet baby was also given a meaningful name. Just
as Hannah in the Old Testament prayed earnestly for her Samuel,
so I prayed for mine. God hears and answers. We prayed Samuel
David would closely listen to God, draw close to Him, and grow
into a man after God's own heart. After all, we were still learning to
listen to God's voice in our lives, but always trying to respond with,
"Here I am, Lord."

My new family of five finally felt complete.

Having three babies in less than four years proved a challenge, but God provided for me in every way. I had friends who
had similar-aged children who would watch mine when I needed
to schedule an appointment while Kevin was out of town, and I
would return the favor for them when they needed assistance. We
were growing our community, but man, was I tired.

I was apparently so tired or distracted for over the next
decade that I never put two and two together until more recently,
near Sammy's 14th birthday, to be exact. My sweet Sammy's earthly birthday was September 12, 2009. My Daisy's heavenly birthday was September 12, 2004. Nineteen years after my miscarriage
and fourteen years after the birth of my youngest child, I had a
much-needed, God-given *"Ah-ha"* moment.

As an educator, I live for those "lightbulb" moments when
a student finally grasps a concept for the first time, not because
it was directly taught to them but because they figured it out for
themselves. It's these Eureka moments that truly fill a teacher's
heart. And my patient Heavenly Rabbi must have been smiling
down when my bulb enlightened.

After so long, I understood! Only God could ordain such
beauty. He is a God of order and not chaos, a God of hope and not
despair. He is a God who blesses those who love Him. We see His
handiwork in nature so easily but sometimes so slowly in our own

lives. He is, after all, the only one who designed it so that a dead tree can become a nurse log for other plants or so that dead plants can become compost and nutrients for new ones to grow. He is the one who arranged for dead animals to become food for scavengers and those scavengers to be the clean-up crew for nature. He is the creator of the water cycle, where evaporation from a body of water becomes the water vapor in the clouds that then precipitates to water the land and refill the bodies of water. He is all about going full circle. And, in our lives, He is the only one who can take a heartache and turn it into a testimony!

This same God was the one who nudged me to complete our family at just the right time so that five years after my miscarriage, I would have a beautiful, healthy child. And it was the same God who was patient with me for the next 14 years even to recognize His meticulous handiwork. He is so loving, so patient, so diligent, so merciful, so wonderful that I'm…just… so…humbled! How could someone so large and powerful who formed the continents, the multitude of stars, and galaxies care for me enough to intricately design my cells and my life's timelines?? It is beyond mind-boggling but also incredibly true.

God turned my mourning into dancing, my tears into shouts of joy! All I can do is faithfully trust Him more and more each day, depend on Him more and more with each decision, and share my testimonies of HIS greatness with anyone who will listen. God completed his full circle, and my writing these words down for you to read will hopefully help you notice all the full circles in your life that God has ordained.

Points to Ponder

1. Looking back, do you notice any scars or heartaches that have become testimonies in your life?

2. Have you ever taken the time to thank God for turning your tears into shouts of joy?

3. If you are in a season of 'tears,' does it encourage you to know that God is preparing the details for your future 'shouts of joy?'

4. Read 1 Samuel Chapters 1 and 2. How can you relate to Hannah's heartfelt prayers and God's divine answers?

Devotion: God Reveals Himself in Unique Ways
Facebook, May 2022

"One must always have a WHY...here's a spiritual lesson from the Appalachian Trail.

While backpacking uphill, Sammy was like, 'WHY are we doing this???!'

I told him that it was a great question and answered with the views, the wild ponies, the time away in nature unplugged, the quality time together, etc.

I went on and on for a good mile of hiking, talking sports psychology, and how 80% of most hard things are mental and only 20% physical—things I have learned along the way from marathon running and other life challenges.

He still didn't have HIS WHY, though.

I finally suggested, 'How about I give you $10 when you make it to the campsite as long as you don't complain the whole way?'

He suggested $20 - the all-time financial negotiator that he is.

I said, 'No, $10.'

But I also reminded him how important it is to challenge yourself to things you can't possibly do on your own because when you reach the end of YOUR strength, you are forced to rely on a higher strength.

If everything was always easy for us, we would never need GOD.

I quoted Isaiah 40:31 and Philippians 4:13 - verses I typically rely on myself.

He was quiet after that. You could tell he was learning and thinking it through (and also trying hard not to complain), and maybe even praying a bit himself.

And in HIS awesomeness, God showed up for this 12-year-old in only a way God can...

Upon entering our campsite, sitting right next to a pile of wild pony manure, Sammy found a crumpled-up $20 bill.

I mean, you can't make this stuff up. We are in the middle of nowhere. Sammy had prayed for strength and a WHY.

He really wanted $20 and not $10.

And God showed up in a way to reveal Himself to my 12-year-old.

God is cool like that.

He meets each of us right where we are in unique ways that only we would understand.

For my son, who needs to learn a bit more about fighting through physical pain with a strong mental game...and who is daily learning to rely on God's strength rather than his own, God showed up with a $20 bill in the middle of the Appalachian Trail.

*Footnote: By the way, this happened well over three years ago. That $20 bill is still tacked to my teenager's bulletin board as a contant reminder of God's unique intervention in his young life. God gave Sammy a priceless gift in that rectangular green piece of paper, one which he will cherish always.

8

"Sloppy Wet Kiss"

"As the Father has loved me, so have I loved you. Now remain in my love." John 15:9 (NIV)

Around the time I was birthing my babies, a beautiful contemporary Christian song called "How He Loves " was released. We sang it often in church, with the original lyrics by John Mark McMillan. The second verse and chorus were......

We are His portion, and He is our prize,
Drawn to redemption by the grace in His eyes,
If grace is an ocean, we're all sinking.
*So, Heaven meets Earth like a **sloppy wet kiss***
And my heart turns violently inside of my chest,
I don't have time to maintain these regrets,
When I think about the way...
He loves us,
Oh! how He loves us,
Oh! how He loves us,
Oh, how He loves.

Christian culture can be nitpicky sometimes, and David Crowder, with McMillian's permission, later changed the above lyrics to "unforeseen kiss" to accommodate those who later changed the above lyrics to were offended by the "sloppiness." Personally, I will always treasure the original lyrics because God used them one beautiful evening to meet me exactly where I was, with exactly what I needed.

As I briefly mentioned earlier, I grew up in a single-parent household. Though divorce rates have been sadly rising for decades, growing up, I didn't know anyone else living in a "broken" home. My father left our family when I was just four years old, and I only saw him sporadically for the next year or so. I don't remember seeing him again until I was about 16 years old. When I was a junior in high school, I simply found his work number and called him. I had wanted and needed a father desperately at that time in my life. Unfortunately, old wounds are hard to heal for all involved. Without going into further detail, let's just say that the daddy-shaped hole in my heart did not get fixed by my earthly father as I had hoped.

As I have already shared, I sought love in the wrong place through an ex-boyfriend who wasn't able to repair my heart either but instead created more scars that needed healing. And though I was now happily married to a Christ-following man, he, too, wasn't able to heal my heart, no matter how hard he tried. A spouse's love was not what my heart needed; instead, it merely served as a band-aid, covering an old wound.

For lack of better words to explain it, the utter rejection of a parent left me with a heart that seemed to have a leak in it. Kevin would pour his love onto me in every love language he could think of, but the love always seemed to drain out before I could really *feel* it. This left me hurting, and Kevin frustrated that his wife was suffering, with his efforts seemingly fruitless.

About the time Sammy was a year old, I found myself incredibly sad. The past year had been challenging. We had three very young children, and Kevin was constantly traveling with his job. in addition, my stepfather died of a massive heart attack, leaving my mom by herself and utterly depressed at the sudden loss of a second husband. She would call often, inadvertently piling her grief onto my chaos. On top of that, our neighbors divorced and moved, and when asked, we somehow agreed to take their hyper puppy, Dude. I was physically, mentally, and emotionally exhausted from it all. One day, while driving, I felt as if I was having my very own heart attack. There was a sharp pain in my chest, making it difficult to breathe. I drove myself to the doctor, and an EKG was performed. My physical heart was apparently fine, but I was diagnosed with anxiety and depression.

The medicine I was prescribed made things worse, so after a few months of trying, I tossed them all, still feeling helpless, hurt, and unhealthy.

But each Sunday, I would cry out to Jesus in worship, soaking up the song "How He Loves." Knowing that God loved me brought me such peace. The problem was a disconnect from my brain to my heart, though. I knew I was loved, but my heart still seemed to be a leaky bucket. I had such a hard time *feeling* that love.

One special night, God healed my leak through my husband's powerful prayer. I remember sitting on our bed after the kids went to bed. I was crying in my sadness, telling Kevin how I still *felt* so unloved. I remember Kevin wrapping his strong arms around me, pulling me into an embrace. As Kevin prayed, the lyrics of "How He Loves" came to my mind and seemed stuck on repeat. I kept hearing those words....

So, Heaven meets Earth like a ***sloppy wet kiss***.
And my heart turns violently inside of my chest,
I don't have time to maintain these regrets,
When I think about, the way...
He loves us.

God loved me. I *knew* it. Kevin loved me. I *knew* that, too. My inner prayer became, "Lord, help me feel it."

Kevin prayed aloud the same words, *"Lord, please just help Holly feel my love and your love for her."* At that exact moment, Dude, unprompted, jumped onto our bed and began to lick my face nonstop. He hadn't been in the room when we sat down. He hadn't been called. It wasn't even in his character to behave like that. It was as if God had supernaturally instructed him to literally cover me with **sloppy wet kisses** so I could truly *feel* how deeply I was loved.

God knew my heart and needs, for He is a God of all wisdom and knowledge.

God heard Kevin and my prayers, for He is a God who listens to His children's cries for help.

God loved me so much, for He is a tender father who loves unconditionally and immensely.

God went to great lengths to show me His love at the exact moment I needed it, for He is a God of minute details.

God even fixed my leaky heart that day, for He is a God of all power.

God knew I would need to fully *comprehend* and *feel* His love so deeply and intensely myself before I could share it with others. Just like an airline attendant instructs passengers to put on their own oxygen masks before assisting others, God knew I needed to heal first so that I could overflow His love to those He placed in my path. I never could have imagined the adventures He had in store for me.

Points to Ponder

1. Read *Psalm 68:5* - what does it say about God being a father to the fatherless? Think about how God has been a loving father to you.

2. Read *Psalm 147:5* - what does it say about God's wisdom and power? Do you fully believe in God's ability to do anything?

3. Read *Psalm 18:6* and *34:17* - what does it say about God's desire and ability to hear your prayers?

4. Has there ever been a time when God used someone, something, or even a song to speak directly to your heart? How did that experience affect you?

Devotion: Beautifully Created

Facebook, December 2018

"Ellie just brought this inside for me, my last rose of the season.

Do you know what a rose is called when it's cold, covered in ice, and the weather is pounding down on it?

A Rose.

The Spiritual implications of this are huge!

Life may beat down on us.

We may feel like the elements are too much to handle.

We may be the only one of our kind still left.

But we are still beautifully created.

And our identity does not depend on the circumstances in life.

So, shake your troubles off and shine your beauty!

"For everything God created is good..." 1 Timothy 4:4 (NIV)

9

A Miracle of Biblical Proportions

"You should remember the words of the Lord Jesus: 'It is more blessed to give than to receive.'" Acts 20:35 (NLT)

Once, when the kids were little, we were all excited to drive to Savannah, Georgia, with Kevin on a tag-a-long work trip. I was even giddy, for I had never been there before and had always heard so many pleasant things about that city. I had spent the week prior planning all sorts of fun activities to keep the kids entertained and educated while Kevin worked. We would spend one day at a nature preserve, another on a boat tour, and more.

The morning we were to leave, I woke up with my Bible near my face. I had fallen asleep the night before while working on my Community Bible Study. So, my notebook and Bible were next to my pillow on the bed. The kids, with all their energy, had also awakened and came bulldozing into our bedroom. All three had climbed onto the bed as Kevin and I began to finish our last-minute packing. The kids then started jumping up and down on the bed in their young excitement while they chatted about hopefully seeing dolphins on the boat tour. In their zeal, they knocked my Bible and notebook onto the floor. I quickly grabbed both, shoved them into my backpack, and asked the kids to hop down. We then proceeded downstairs for a quick breakfast before heading out the door to Savannah.

The next morning, after breakfast with Daddy at the hotel, we hopped in the van and followed GPS directions to the nature preserve. The kids and I hiked for about ten minutes when the skies suddenly opened, and we were forced to run back to the van for cover.

I was disappointed and drenched. I didn't know this city, and I had only planned outdoor activities. I hadn't planned for rain, nor did I know what to do next. But the one thing I did know was that I refused to take three energetic kids back to the hotel room for the next nine hours.

In this moment of stress, I said a quick prayer something like, "*Lord, I have made all these plans without you. Please forgive me. Please guide the kids and I today to be in your perfect will. Where would you have us go? What would you have us do? Please direct us. Amen.*"

I lifted my head out of prayer, turned to face the kids in the backseat, and said, "Mommy just asked God where we are to go next."

One of them asked, "Can we go get some hot chocolate? I'm cold and wet from the rain."

I thought, "Okay. Maybe I can think and pray more while the kids get something warm to drink." I Googled the closest place to the nature preserve and found that there was a small diner nearby, so we drove there.

The kids and I sat in a booth and ordered our hot chocolates. As we waited, a couple in the booth next to ours engaged in a heated discussion. I overheard things like, "You need to pay more attention to your teen daughter." Apparently, the couple was divorced and had met over coffee to discuss co-parenting their child. Suddenly frustrated with the conversation, the ex-husband stormed out of the restaurant, leaving the woman looking down at her cup of coffee.

I instantly knew that God had directed us to this exact place at this moment. I waited a moment and mustered up the courage. I leaned over to the lady and said, *"Mam, I couldn't help but notice that you are having a rough day. I would like to buy you coffee. And it's just my kids and me here. Would you want to join us in our booth?"*

Thankfully, she accepted and slid over with us. The kids were busy coloring and talking together, and I was able to chat with the woman. I learned that her teenager was really struggling with the fact that her father wasn't keeping promises to her. The poor mother wasn't sure how to help her daughter and the depression that it was causing her.

My experience growing up without a father was a blessing at this particular moment. I was able to tell this struggling mother that I could relate to her daughter. God created a scenario where this woman was open to hearing how God filled the daddy-shaped hole in my heart. I suggested she read *Jeremiah 29:11 (NIV)* to her daughter. I quoted it for her, ***"For I know the plans I have for you," declares the Lord, "plans to prosper you and not to harm you, plans to give you hope and a future."***

I was so convinced that this verse was what God wanted this woman to hear at that moment and then share with her daughter that I suggested, *"Just go home and read it to her tonight."*

The lady looked at me and sheepishly replied, *"But I don't own a Bible."*

This! This was what God wanted of me, I thought! *"Mam, that's ok. I packed my Bible with me on this trip. It is right in the van. The kids are done with their drinks. Why don't I pay, and you can walk out with us? I would be honored to give you and your daughter my Bible."*

Hope for the first time in a long time must have flooded this woman's heart. She eagerly accepted the invitation, and I saw her smile for the first time. The five of us walked out to the parking lot. It was suddenly sunny out now. At the van, I opened the back, reached into my backpack, grabbed my Bible, and handed over a book packed with Love, Hope, and Truth to this mother. She thanked me but said, *"I really don't know where to start reading, though."*

"Oh, that's easy. This has been my Bible for years. I have already underlined and highlighted some of the best parts. Start there. And, here, I'll put the bookmark at Jeremiah 29 for you."

As the woman started to drive away, I felt perfectly in the center of God's will. My heart was full, and there was a huge smile on my face. But then, I realized something, and my flesh complained to God, *"But God, that was MY Bible. I mean, it had MY family tree written in the front."*

Instantly, God spoke to my selfishness, and I heard Him gently reply, **"The Word of God is for all my children. Do not worry."**

So, I didn't, and I chose to trust God. The kids and I enjoyed the next few days exploring Savannah, with dinners and breakfast with Daddy each day. Then we all drove home. I occasionally thought of the Savannah mama and said a quiet prayer for her and her daughter.

When we pulled into the driveway at home, I wasn't thinking of anything besides unpacking the van, starting a load of laundry, and eventually crashing into my bed. We unlocked the door, and I carried my bag up to my bedroom. When I walked in, my eyes spotted something on the floor, and tears flooded my eyes. Lying right there, next to my bed on the floor, was my Family Tree. Apparently, when the kids jumped on my bed the morning we left, and my Bible fell to the floor, it must have fallen out, and in my haste to pack and leave, I hadn't noticed. Or perhaps some angel deposited it for me for my act of trust and obedience by giving my Bible away. I'll never know, and it doesn't matter. I know that God heard my heart. The only few pieces of that book that were truely mine were given back to me. The rest of the pages were God's Words to all. It was a miracle of Biblical proportions. Had I not experienced it, I may not even believe it myself.

God's powerful presence that week changed me. I studied God's Word intensely. I also discovered how I could get it on my phone and read it in different versions.

A year or two later, during Community Bible Study, I shared this story with my group. I think I mentioned it in explaining why I no longer used a paper Bible. The next week, a sweet friend of mine gifted me with a brand-new study Bible. She told me that she would pray that I would read, underline, highlight it, and then share it with someone else.

Since that miraculous time, I never once saw a Bible as mine anymore. (I also stopped filling out the Family Tree pages.) I read through my new gifted Bible over the next few years and attended more classes of Community Bible Study. I wrote all in it and eventually gifted it to Ellie. I wanted her to always know how much her mama loved God and his Word. I then bought another, read through it, and gifted it to my kidney recipient - which you'll read more about in a few chapters. I then bought another and gave it to Ben on his 16th birthday.

I bought another with the intention of gifting it to Sammy for his 16th birthday, but God had other plans. Sheila's son, Damien, who now goes by "LJ," as he was called by his father during his childhood, came to visit us. He is now 22 and in the army. He hadn't grown up with much exposure to the Christian faith. One Sunday, I offered him to use my Bible when he attended church with us. The sermon was on Hebrews 9, so I turned my Bible to that section for LJ. After the service, LJ told us that during an altar call, he had wanted to stand up but couldn't bring himself to, so he looked down at my Bible he was holding. It had miraculously shifted a few pages to Hebrews 11, which I had already underlined at a previous time. His eyes caught the verse,

"Now faith is confidence in what we hope for and assurance about what we do not see."

God's Word is alive and living! LJ stood there, flabbergasted at the miracle. I asked him if he owned a Bible, to which he replied that he didn't. I smiled and told him to keep the one he was holding. He initially tried to refuse, saying, *"But you have already written in this one and have your own notes."*

This was the perfect time to recount to him the story of which you just read how God has performed miracles and how I purposefully write in my Bibles, knowing that God will instruct me to give them to someone else one day.

After church that day, I ordered a new Bible and am now reading it and marking it up for Sammy's 16th birthday—or for whomever God wants this one to go to.

Ellie, who is now a junior in college, purposefully began praying over her Bible, knowing that the Lord wanted her to gift it to someone, and she was so confident in that calling that she even wrote prayers for the future recipient in the cover. While Ellie was home on summer break, we had some friends over for dinner. That night we discovered that one particular woman in her 20's, a new believer, was in need of a study Bible. I offered to buy her one on Amazon, but Ellie ran upstairs and came back down with a huge smile on her face. She gifted her Bible to this new believer in front of me. We were all crying as we learned the details; Ellie had started writing in the Bible and praying over its recipient the same week this young woman got baptized months before. God wanted this young believer to have my daughter's Bible. As a mama, I was so proud of my daughter and her faithfulness to trust and obey. As a friend, I was happy to see this new young believer experience God's divine provision for her. As a child of God, I was reminded how God clearly cares for each one of His children.

God's Word is designed for all, and He will make sure those

who need it get it. But God is also a God who sees and cares about His children. He cared about the daughter whose father was neglecting her. He cared about a mother who didn't know how to fill the daddy-shaped hole in her daughter's heart. He cared about a young man who had grown up without a mother and was seeking Him for the first time. He cared about a young woman who desired to study His Word more in-depth. He cared about my own daughter who needed to experience the blessing of trusting and obeying for herself. He cared about me and growing my faith exponentially. He cares.

That day in Savannah, I didn't just learn to be generous, but I learned to fully trust and obey. It was like my life was a video game, and I leveled up that day. I saw God work miracles, and with that, my faith powered up. God was slowly and patiently teaching me to trust and to be generous with those things that were nearest and dearest to me.

Points to Ponder

1. Do you believe in miracles? If so, why do you think God allows some sometimes but not others?

2. Have you ever read through the entire Bible? If not, what's been stopping you? If yes, what have been some of the blessings from reading God's Word in its entirety?

3. Would you ever give away your Bible or something that is special to you if you thought it could help someone else experience the love of Jesus?

Devotion: Turning Family Vacations into Mission Trips
Facebook, March 2015

"I posted a ton of pics from our recent trip to DC, but my favorite moments weren't captured with a camera. Times when my children used THEIR souvenir money (that they withdrew from their savings at home and brought with them) to give to the homeless they saw in need.

A time when they were cold and saw a homeless man who looked cold, and they used their money to buy him a hot chocolate. (And the deep sense of appreciation in his eyes when they walked it over to him.)

When they packed a dozen brown bag lunches, decorated the bags with scripture verses and smiley faces and hearts, and THEY carried them all around for miles of walking in D.C. just in case they saw a homeless person to give one to.

And the times when they handed them out, approaching these strangers with tender love and childlike faith (with mommy and daddy close by for safety, of course).

Times when they would be in the middle of running and playing and hear an ambulance siren, and huddle together to pray for whoever was in need.

It's ironic because before we traveled, I called a couple D.C. area homeless shelters, halfway houses, and domestic abuse shelters, asking if we could come by one day of the trip to volunteer because there are so many people in need in that area. ALL said that volunteers had to be at least 16 years old and trained in advance. So, we prayed that God would put those He wanted us to serve in our paths. And He did.

Precious memories I don't want to forget. And memories I don't share with an attitude of pride but with an attitude of encouragement. My prayer is that more Christ followers would look forward to serving those in need and willingly and sacrificially give of their time, energy, and money to help those in need around them. This world would be a completely different place if Christians would really love like Jesus loved.

"My friends, what good is it to say you have faith, when you don't do anything to show that you really do have faith? Can that kind of faith save you? If you know someone who doesn't have any clothes or food, you shouldn't just say, "I hope all goes well for you. I hope you will be warm and have plenty to eat." What good is it to say this, unless you do something to help? Faith that doesn't lead us to do good deeds is all alone and dead!" James 2:14-17 (CEV)

10

Get Up and Run

"This is my command—be strong and courageous! Do not be afraid or discouraged. For the Lord your God is with you wherever you go." Joshua 1:9 (NLT)

One December when the children were quite young (and before I was a runner!) I read the book "Kisses from Katie." It's a story about a young lady who travels to Uganda to become a missionary, and she ends up changing the world for countless orphans. When I first read her book, I viewed her as a modern-day "Mother Teresa."

Late one night, when everyone was asleep, I curled up in bed under lots of covers and finished the last chapter of her book. Then, I prayed, pouring out my heart to God. I wanted to be a missionary! And I wanted God to change Kevin's heart and have him wake up the next day, turn over, and say, *"Let's move to Uganda!"*

Katie's story inspired me because she acted on her faith. She lived it when it was difficult, and she lived that faith radically. She was changing people's trajectories by living her life on a mission. And I didn't want one more day of my own life to be lived without her kind of radical faith.

I simply thought I might have to move to Uganda or some

other foreign country to be radical. Being married meant I needed Kevin to think and behave radically, too. So, I fervently prayed that God would change Kevin, change his heart and making him more radical and mission-focused. And after I prayed my "Amen," I drifted away to sleep...

Around 3:00 am, I awoke. Or, saying I was awakened would be more accurate. The voice wasn't audible, and there were no shining beams from the heavens alighting my bed. But I heard. My heart heard the words clearly. And I knew exactly WHO was speaking to me. I had heard this "voice" a few times before.

The voice clearly spoke, *"Holly, get up and run."*

Even though I knew it was God, and even though I knew it was a command that I should instantly obey, I apparently am a bit dense. Or maybe too logical.

I replied in my heart, though it seemed just as real as if it were an audible conversation, *"But, Lord, it is 3 am outside! It is dark! I don't even run. Why? This makes no sense! And what will Kevin think if he wakes up while I am gone? Did I mention it's COLD out there!"*

And the voice patiently repeated, *"Holly, get up and run."*

I must have sounded like a whiny child being asked to do her chores by her father because I replied again with the question, *"Do I have to??"*

And the voice once again quietly commanded, *"Holly, get up and run."*

Third time's a charm, some say. Or perhaps I was worried about a third strike getting me out. But this time, I at least considered the words. The inkling of obedience began to take shape in my brain. But my logical human brain also kicked in. I could do this if God were asking it of me, but on the other hand, I am not stupid. I grew up in East Baltimore after all, I know better than to go running alone in the dark. A lone female can attract all kinds of dangers. I thought I was at least taking my big, black dog with me! He could protect me from all the imaginary dangers I conjured up! You know, the dozen rapists who lurked in my middle-class suburban neighborhood, the pack of wolves or coyotes who resided down by the stop sign, the rabid raccoons across the street from the community clubhouse. My list of imaginable dangers quickly formed in my brain.

So, I said, "*Ok, God. I will run.*" And then I called out to our sleeping pet, "*Come on, Dude!*"

Dude's ears perked up out of his dreamy state. He even tilted his head at me in canine confusion, wondering about my out-of-the-ordinary, middle-of-the-night behavior.

But God stopped me. And if the voice had been audible, it would have been a few notches louder than the initial commands,

"**No!**" And then it quietly reprimanded, "**If I am for you, who can be against you?**"

At the reminder of the Romans 8:31 passage, I conceded. "*Ok, God. You are right. If the God of the universe is asking me to go for a run in the middle of the night, just the two of us, can I not trust Him enough to protect me during it?*"

To take a quick intermission from my story, I want to focus on this last thought. This was a game-changer for me. But this realization also changed my attitude towards most of the other assignments God has given me since that night.

If God has asked me to do something, then I must have faith that He will protect me during the "doing" of whatever that something is.

I either have faith or I don't. There's no riding the fence. Years later, I would come back to this when my family went on various mission trips to Central America. I would come back to this when asked to serve the homeless. I would come back to this when God asked me to give up an organ for a stranger. This realization is what built my faith.

I have since been asked, *"How can I get as much faith as you?"* But that is NOT the right question to ask. We, humans, often see faith as a percentage. We see Mother Teresa and Billy Graham as people with 99% faith. We see our pastors as having roughly 70-80%. And you may see yourself as only having about 2% on a good day.

But faith is either present or not. You either have it or you don't. It's not something you can quantify with a *"how much"* question. It requires a "yes" or "no" answer. Do you have faith? Yes or no. You either make Jesus the Lord of your life, or you decide to trust in your own abilities.

Some days, you may waver. You might forget who is in charge. It doesn't mean you don't have faith. You simply did not choose it at that moment. It is a continual process. And Jesus reminds us of this in Matthew.

"Then Jesus went to work on his disciples. "Anyone who intends to come with me has to let me lead. You're not in the driver's seat; I am. Don't run from suffering; embrace it. Follow me and I'll show you how. Self-help is no help at all. Self-sacrifice is the way, my way, to finding yourself, your true self. What kind of deal is it to get everything you want but lose yourself? What could you ever trade your soul for?" Matthew 16:24-26 (MSG)

Returning to my story, once I told Dude he could go back to sleep, I started bundling up and tying my sneakers for my impromptu twilight exercise date with my Father. I was all in, perhaps a little groggy, but all in.

As I stepped outside and walked to the end of our short driveway, I asked God, *"Ok, Lord, now what? Which way should I go?"*

"Start jogging down the street." So, I did.

You may be familiar with the New Testament account of Saul's conversion on the Road to Damascus. After seeing Jesus and being blinded for three days, the Lord sent Ananias to pray over Saul. *Acts 9:17-18 (NIV)* says....

"Then Ananias went to the house and entered it. Placing his hands on Saul, he said, 'Brother Saul, the Lord—Jesus, who appeared to you on the road as you were coming here—has sent me so that you may see again and be filled with the Holy Spirit.' Immediately, something like scales fell from Saul's eyes, and he could see again..."

As I began jogging down my street, it was as if my own scales had finally fallen off. I began to look at my neighbors' houses in a new way. All the past conversations with neighbors at the community pool, while out walking the dogs, while watching the kids play at the local playground, or while chatting at the mailbox in the afternoon came flooding back to me. In an instant, I finally understood.

While I jogged down my street, I first noticed the house of an elderly widow on our street. Then I spotted the house of the couple I knew was filing for divorce. As I turned the corner to the next street, I focused on the house of the man who was dying of cancer. And as I continued, I prayed for each of these neighbors and their difficult circumstances.

And as I prayed, I heard God give me my personal commission, *"Holly, THIS is your Uganda!"*

His sweet words spoke to my heart, reminding me of my prayer before I fell asleep the night before. I had wanted to wake up and become a missionary family on fire for Christ. I wanted to share the love of our Savior with the world. I wanted to make a difference in the lives of others.

God answered my prayer that night. And as God so often does, He answered my prayer HIS WAY, not the way I had intended or expected, but in His more divine, perfect way. He had moved Kevin, Ellie, and me here to this neighborhood back in 2007 after months of praying over where to move. And then He blessed us with Ben and Sammy shortly after. Our family was divinely placed in this exact location to do God's will. He had been preparing us for "our mission" the whole time.

We didn't need to sell all our worldly possessions, move across the sea, and live in a third-world country to share the love of Jesus with people who NEEDED to hear the message of hope. We simply needed to walk outside and start talking with our neighbors.

Perspective matters. Identity matters. I wasn't seeing my neighbors as "needy," nor did I think of myself as a "missionary." I was looking at my community and myself through a worldly lens, not through God's eyes. Before that twilight run, I saw middle-class wealth, not starving children. I noticed security, not insecurity. I looked at people with painted-on smiling faces, not souls terrified about their future.

I think I also saw our family as unequipped to do mission work. Kevin and I have degrees in science and education, not theology, after all. I incorrectly thought people needed to be sent somewhere by a structured missional organization before they could be witnesses. My identity needed to shift again.

When we continue to look at the world through an earthly lens, we will inevitably conform to it, subconsciously or not. Saul, who later became known as Paul, reminds us:

>*"Do not conform to the pattern of this world, but be transformed by the renewing of your mind. Then you will be able to test and approve what God's will is—his good, pleasing and perfect will." Romans 12:2 (NIV)*

Returning to my story, I finished my lap around our neighborhood (untouched by those imaginary rabid raccoons, I might add!) and I looked up to the heavens and smiled. *"Thank you, God! I get it! You have placed us here for such a time as this. My mission field is all around me! Yes, the scales are gone, and I can finally see my neighbors as you see them. Thank you! Now, I think I will head home and still catch a little bit of sleep before the kids get up."*

"Not so fast."

Hopefully, I didn't sound like an eye-rolling teenager unenthusiastically working at the local burger joint. But I did reply to God and ask, *"Now what?"* as I released an unnecessary amount of air from my lungs.

"I need you to go wake up Kevin and ask for $1000."

"WHAT?!?!" I simply could not fathom where God was headed with this.

"You asked to be a missionary family. Kevin needs to know what's going on. And my children - your neighbors - need

tangible evidence that I love them and will provide for them. I want you to give anonymously $100 to ten of your neighbors, your mission field."

Thankfully, I didn't argue with God nearly as much as his first request to get up and run. But I still hesitated. I mean, what on earth will my husband think when I wake him up, tell him that I have been out running, alone (with those rabid raccoons, by the way), in the middle of the night. AND, oh, by the way, God wants us to drain our emergency savings account and just anonymously give it away to a few local mailboxes.........

When I tell this story to friends, I often insert a joke here. I laughingly say that I must have had a transfiguration glow about me when I woke Kevin up that night. He must have visibly noticed that I had just spent time with the Creator Himself. Because in his cool, calm, collected way, Kevin simply responded with, *"Ok."*

My husband is a man of few words. He has a strong faith in God, but he also has faith in his wife's faith. And when I rambled out my middle-of-the-night story at hyper speed, it was like a very long run-on sentence....

"Wake up, Kev! Wake up! God got me up a bit ago and told me to go running, And I did, and my scales are gone, and I can see, and did you know that the widow on our street must be very lonely, and the neighbors are divorcing, and the poor guy down on the corner, he doesn't have much time left, and his poor wife must be distraught, and I don't know why I never noticed all this before, but this is our Uganda!! This is our Uganda!!! AAAAANNNNDDDDD by the way, God wants us to give ten of our neighbors each $100. That's $1,000. Today. Ok?!?!?"

"Ok."

"Did you hear me? $1000! It's our emergency savings

account! And it's only two weeks before Christmas. You are ok with this?"

"Ok."

"We need to write out ten Christmas cards, withdraw $1000 from the bank when it opens later, and then under the cover of darkness anonymously deliver these cards, each with $100 in them, to our neighbors' mailboxes. You are ok with this??"

Kevin looked at me with his dark, handsome, stoic eyes, and quietly said, *"If God has told you we need to do this, then ok."* Simple as that. That's my man. God had been growing his faith all those years as well.

In your mental image of how this night was unfolding for me, you can now insert a sappy wife hugging her beloved husband and quietly thanking God that he isn't calling the local mental health hospital to have her screened after her recent odd behavior!

God had clearly pointed out the fact that we were to bless ten neighbors. However, he had only laid five of those on my heart. This is where God further unified my husband and me on our family's mission. I told Kev that he needed to pray about the other five. And he did. Sure enough, throughout that day, God laid on his heart the remaining mailboxes that were in for a divine surprise.

Dude was happy the following night. He was able to go for a walk with me as I delivered the surprises. Each card had a $100 bill and a simple note from the Luke Christmas story.

"But the angel said to them, 'Do not be afraid. I bring you good news that will cause great joy for all the people. Today in the town of David a Savior has been born to you; he is the Messiah, the Lord.'" Luke 2:10-11 NIV

Meanwhile, Kevin took over the kids' bedtime routines. The Armstrong family had completed their first official divine mission.

It felt so freeing to give so generously. It felt so accepting to be trusted with such a task. It felt so joyful, simply joyful, to bring other great news - joyful news that was for all people - not just Ugandans, but my neighbors here in South Carolina.

I will admit that a few doubts started to creep in. Over the next few days, Satan started to whisper them to me. And every time, I handed those doubts over to God. I knew I heard from God, for there was no denying that. I knew He wanted us to give the money away. It was almost like God wanted us to have an opportunity to put our faith into action. Faith without works is dead, after all, according to James 2. So, what was I doubting? Did we give the right amount? Did we give to the right people?

God hears our anxieties. He hears us. He cares. He answers.

A few days later, I ran into a friend of mine. She was one of the five neighbors that God had laid on my heart. She and I had been talking about Jesus over the last few months. She had been living with her boyfriend of many years, and they had three children together. They had recently started going to church and realized they should probably get married. She told me that they had decided one day to finally get their marriage license. They didn't want to be living "in sin" any longer. They didn't tell anyone about it beforehand, and this conversation was the first I was learning.

I asked her which day they married. It was the same day God woke me up in the wee hours of the morning and when I delivered the cards that same evening. I got tears in my eyes as I realized the profound impact of what I had just heard. This couple, who had just decided to take a step of faith and marry, must have driven home from the courthouse to check their mail that night to find a wedding present from God Himself! No one else would have known to give them a wedding present. But God knew. He cared. And He used humble, lowly me to be his hands and feet that day. Now, that was something to be excited about! I congratulated my friend on her wedding. She didn't mention her card and money, and neither did I.

About a week after my run with Dude, I heard about one more anonymous card recipient. Through our pastor, I learned that the widow on the street had been praying for extra grocery money for when her family came over for the holidays. She was praising God when an unexpected answer arrived in her mailbox one evening.

God gave me two confirmations. Not just one, but two. How about that, Satan!?!? No more doubting! And I look forward to Heaven when I learn about the other eight stories and how God intervened in my family's life to meet someone else's private needs.

As I wrap up this chapter, I just want to remind you of the big picture of this story; perhaps it will resonate with you.

- One day, I *read* a book that inspired me to act out my faith more.
- So, I *prayed*, and God answered by speaking to me and giving me a specific task.
- I made the active choice to *obey*, regardless of the cost.
- Then, God blessed....

  ◻Ten neighbors with an unexpected tangible gift.

  ◻Prayerfully, each one on a spiritual level as well; I have faith this is the case.

  ◻Our family, for this, changed our identity, vision, perspectives, and trajectory from that day forward.

  ◻Lastly, hopefully, you for having *read* these words. I pray that you are stirred to *pray* your own prayer, and may you have the courage to *obey* whatever is asked of you so that the cycle of *blessing* continues until the whole world knows about our Lord and Savior!

In case you are wondering, it has been about thirteen years now. In the rough draft of this book, I wrote about how God hadn't divinely instructed me to tell any of the recipients who received surprise monetary gifts that December night so long ago. And I had planned to continue to keep God's secret. However, while editing the rough draft of this chapter, I strongly felt God instructing me to call the neighbor who received her wedding present from God.

And just like I had many years ago, I had to trust God yet again that His timing and ways were always perfect. I wasn't sure how to make that phone call, for I was content with keeping it anonymous, but I have learned enough over the years not to argue with God. I spoke to my neighbor about that time in her life when she married and if she remembered receiving anything in the mail. She instantly recalled the card and money and said through teary eyes, *"That money was such a blessing at a time when we needed it most. I really felt God's favor."*

In addition, she commented how she had recently been feeling far from God, and how someone had invited her to join their small group and attend the very night I called. She admitted to being initially hesitant, but after our conversation, she commented, *"I feel God wants me to grow closer to Him again. I think I'll go to that group tonight!"*

This was music to my ears. God never ceases to amaze me. God perfectly timed the card all those years ago, as well as my recent phone call. We all need to be tuned in and willing to obey whatever He commands of us. Sometimes, He may ask radical things like running in the middle of the night and donating large sums of money, and other times, He may simply want us to pick up the phone. When we trust and obey, not only do we draw closer to God, but others could as well.

Points to Ponder

1. Have you ever heard the voice of God asking you to do something radical? If so, how did you respond?

2. Have you ever prayed for God to change someone else's
mindset and then He showed you that it was YOURS all the
time that needed changing?

3. What does Joshua 1:9 mean to you right now in your life?
*"This is my command—be strong and courageous! Do not
be afraid or discouraged. For the Lord your God is with you
wherever you go." Joshua 1:9 (NLT)*

Devotion: Be Plugged into the Correct Source
Facebook, March 2023

A lot of the Bible is written in agricultural parables and analogies because that was the culture at the time it was written—it talks about sheep, vineyards, and herds of cattle.

Well, God gave me a great modern visual of John 15:5 this morning as I was getting ready for the day.

I disconnected my phone from its charging cord near my bed to turn on some music while I did my hair and makeup.

But I instantly noticed that I had the red warning signal that my battery was low.

How could it be?? I plugged it in last night!!

Then I saw that the charging cord that was connected to my phone was NOT also connected to the wall, the source of power...

Is this you in your life today?

Are you running around on what feels like an empty battery, about to shut down at any minute?

And it's not from lack of trying!

But if where you are attempting to get your energy is NOT plugged into the RIGHT source, you will continue to drain...

Just a spiritual point to ponder this morning - where are you trying to connect that isn't actually filling you up, helping you become the best version of yourself?

Maybe it's time to reevaluate all connections...

"I am the vine; you are the branches. If you remain in me and I in you, you will bear much fruit; APART FROM ME YOU CAN DO NOTHING." John15:5 (NIV)

11

Marathon Training

"Have you never heard? Have you never understood? The Lord is the everlasting God, the Creator of all the earth. He never grows weak or weary. No one can measure the depths of his understanding. He gives power to the weak and strength to the powerless. Even youths will become weak and tired, and young men will fall in exhaustion. But those who trust in the Lord will find new strength. They will soar high on wings like eagles. They will run and not grow weary. They will walk and not faint."
Isaiah 40:28-31 (NLT)

I'm a self-confessed Type A overachiever "wannabe." When I choose to do something, I'm all in, and I want to give whatever it is 110%. Not until I sat to start writing did I realize how much our late dog, Dude, would be in this book. In previous chapters, I wrote about how difficult life was during the early years of parenting and how we weren't looking for another dog. Still, Dude had come to us when Sammy was only six months old, throwing me a curve ball with one more living creature to take care of. Dude had a lot of energy. And I mean a lot! He was a border collie mix and insisted on 'herding' the children as they ran around the yard playing, nipping at their heels. It was frustrating for them and for me.

After the night God woke me up and told me to run our neighborhood, I decided that perhaps running should be part of my regular routine. I soon realized that if I took Dude with me, even for just two miles, we could all tolerate his energy a bit more. Little did I know that running his energy out each morning would inspire me to the next level of trusting and obeying God.

My heart wanted to be a missionary, but God had told me that I was already in my mission field, "My Uganda." So, I began running prayer laps around my neighborhood with Dude in tow. Friends realized that I was running a lot, and some joined me for morning runs. One of those friends wanted to train for a half marathon. I quickly liked the idea and soon started training, too. The unique thing about me was that I had never even run a 5K before, not one single race. But I realized that running was beneficial for my mental health, to be outside every morning, sweat a little, and spend time in nature. I would either spend time with God if I ran alone or time with friends if I ran with others. This exercise routine made me a better wife and mother. And if you know a runner or are one yourself, you might know how addicting it can become.

In my half marathon training one Saturday, I went out on a long run, hoping to complete 8-10 miles. I had music blasting in my ears (most likely Toby Mac since he's been a favorite musical running companion of mine for years). As I was running, I became busy talking to God, mentally singing along with Toby, and just placing one foot in front of the other. I didn't check my phone for mileage along the way, but by the time I had finished, I realized I had run 15 miles! I couldn't believe it. I began thinking, *"A half marathon is only 13.1 miles; I have already proven I could run that. Should I just go ahead and train for a full marathon at 26.2?"*

I chatted with Kevin to make sure he would approve and that I wasn't biting off more than I could chew. He, who has always been my biggest cheerleader, encouraged me to go for it. So, I picked up another running buddy who was also training for a full marathon, and we began running together every morning before dawn. (With both of us having young children, we had to be home by the time our husbands needed to leave for work.)

A buddy made all the difference, and we encouraged each other. But I knew I needed a deeper WHY for this training. Why was I doing this again? I didn't want to run this race for me, for it would be too easy to quit when it inevitably became difficult. At the time, our church supported a group of orphans in Kenya, Africa. I knew that if I began raising money for those orphans as part of my marathon training, I would find that deeper motivation outside of myself. This would also fulfill my inner desire for mission work. If God wouldn't send me to a foreign country, I could at least send funds along with the missionaries who were sent. I ended up fundraising $1000 to send to Kenya.

I also quickly realized that my body HURT during and after long runs. It would be quintessential that I learned to rely on a higher power for the strength and endurance to complete this monumental task. One morning during my quiet time, I came across Isaiah 40, the verses quoted at the very beginning of this chapter. God never grows tired or weak. People do, but God never does. And those who trust in God can tap into God's strength; He can carry them along when their bodies are weak. This was pivotal for me. I knew I couldn't run this race without Him.

I hadn't even really considered myself a runner or an athlete yet. I was just someone who began getting the wiggles out of a dog and then realized that I, too, had wiggles that needed to be worked out each morning. I was merely a young mom who discovered that 60-90 minutes outside of the house without my three beautiful appendages each morning was better than only 20 minutes. I felt like an individual again, a child of God, a human being who had her own aspirations and personal goals, not "just a mom." I also wanted to show my children, through my example, that *"Yes, we can do hard things, as long as we trust in God and and in His will for our lives!"*

For four months, I trained. We started training in the heat and humidity of a South Carolina summer. We ended our training in the cold mornings of November. Unfortunately, never having trained this hard before, I still had so much to learn about letting your body rest, dressing appropriately for all sorts of weather, fueling properly, and so much more. The week before race day, I found myself sick. Then, in the days leading up to the big day, I became sicker, ending up with bronchitis.

Whether this was Satan trying to deter me from my accomplishments, God trying to teach me to tap into His strength more, or just my own ignorance in health and nutrition, I don't really know, but I decided that I was *not* NOT going to run that race. I had trained too hard already, and the orphans were relying on me. The donors of the funds were expecting me to compete. I simply needed to rely on God to sustain me.

The morning of the race, at the starting line, I found myself freezing and hacking. I began running alongside my buddy, who had fortunately stayed healthy. But by about mile 11, not even halfway through, I encouraged her to run ahead without me. I didn't want to hold her back from being the best she could be.

The first half of the race was in a crowded area with a large fan base. People lined the streets of the neighborhoods we ran through, holding signs, cheering on the runners, and sharing their energy with the tired racers. But the second half of the race weaved us through the industrial part of Charlotte with very little fan support. I found myself cold, tired, sick, hurting, alone. But I kept one foot going in front of the other.

I continually repeated the Isaiah verses as my mantra, *"But those who trust in the Lord will find **new strength**. They will **soar** high on wings like eagles. They will **run** and not grow weary. They will walk and **not faint."**

I could not have completed that race without the strength

of my Lord. I ran and never walked. Sure, I grew tired, but I never grew too weary to stop. I felt like God rose me above the trials of the asphalt and soared me to my first-ever finish line.

I became a runner that day, and not just a runner, but a marathoner. But more importantly, I became one who trusted her body with her Lord, one who never doubted that when my body hurt, God would heal me. When my body grew tired, God would give me energy. When my body ached, God would sustain me. Learning these truths that day in 2012 taught me to depend on God for everything. It taught me to live for more than myself. It taught me that completing hard things was possible. It taught me to face large obstacles with faith and simply trust in God for strength.

I learned a phrase that autumn. It was "Kwa watoto," which in Swahili means "For the children." I even wrote it on my hand with a Sharpie so I could remember that I ran not for myself but for the sake of others. This motherly mentality and sacrificial love for others is exactly what God would use to draw me into the idea of kidney donation eight years later.

Between that first marathon and the time I donated, I ran another full marathon and countless half-marathons, 5Ks and 10Ks. I even dragged Kevin out for a half-marathon for our 13th wedding anniversary because it's just natural to ask your non-running husband to run 13 miles when your 13th anniversary is October 13th, right?! He loved me enough to run it like a champ and even completed a full marathon with me the following year.

And in case you are wondering about our sweet Dude - we ended up getting him a shepherd-mix puppy named Maggie for him to herd instead of the kids. It was a perfect fit. He wasn't exactly built for running distance miles with me, and he, unfortunately, developed a disease that stole him from us at the young age of 7 years old. Maggie, however, was lean and sleek and could run for hours and hours. She would rise to be my faithful running buddy for 12 years, earning some of her own 5K and half marathon medals. We recently had to lay her down, but her little sister, Sadie (who is *not* built for running), is now my walking buddy as I still take prayer walks around our "Uganda."

Points to Ponder

1. Have you ever attempted a radically large goal, knowing that you could only achieve it with God's help and
   not by your own strength? How did that experience ele-
   vate your faith? If you haven't, perhaps pray that God creates an opportunity for you to begin relying on Him more.

2. Read *Isaiah 40:28-31*. What are the truths about God in that
   passage? Do you trust God enough to strengthen you in your
   most exhausting circumstances?

Devotion - Soar like an Eagle

Written as part of a Community Bible Study Devotional, circa 2017

"Growing up, I didn't always feel secure or loved. After all, I didn't have the normal parental love speaking into my life. Dad was gone. Mom was in and out emotionally. I always felt alone. I felt like a baby duck who wasn't being shown how to fly. This really affected me as a parent. The devil would taunt me and feed me doubts about my ability to raise my kids effectively. I will admit to listening to these doubts way more than I should have. But God... He always intervenes.

In 2016, I was especially feeling like an orphaned duck. I was flapping around, quacking my complaints and never feeling like I could take off and fly. I carried so much doubt. I seemed to be making so many parenting mistakes. I felt like I was drowning instead of flying.

But I spent time with God...and God brought to my attention the verse in Isaiah that says, "Those who trust in the Lord will renew their strength and they will soar on wings like eagles."

God told me, "*Holly, you are an eagle, not a duck. See yourself as I see you, as I designed you.*"

The story of the Ugly Duckling came to mind. You see, I had my identity all wrong. I believed I was a failure, doomed for failure because my childhood wasn't the best. But God showed me that I was an eagle. And eagles soar. They don't flap. In fact, God designed eagles to sense oncoming storms and rise above them. They are not meant to flap through them.

And eagles mate for life. I never had to worry about my children also growing up in a broken home like I did because God sent me Kevin, my mate for life.

In fact, it was such a revolutionary identity change - thinking of myself as an eagle rather than a duck - that Kevin bought me an eagle sculpture chiseled out of marble that Christmas. To this day, it is one of the most meaningful and thoughtful presents he has ever given me.

Being the crybaby that I am, tears came to my eyes as I held this marvelous work of art. Kevin was reaffirming my identity and cheering me on as I soared. He didn't think I was quacking and flapping around like a duck. He saw me as God saw me. And that was so important. God believed in me. My mate believed in me. I had to believe in myself. We even went together and bought a second eagle, so the original had its mate by its side constantly.

As I marveled at these eagles and the sharp chisel lines in their rock, God showed me another important truth. Sometimes, the shaping and refining process doesn't feel good—it feels painful. But God is simply chiseling us into the beings He has designed us to be.

Don't resist the master sculptor. He has a plan! Spend time with the artist, ask Him questions about his work of art, find out his plan, and watch and be amazed at the beautiful creation He forms!

12

Homeschool

"Direct your children onto the right path, and when they are older, they will not leave it." **Proverbs 22:6 (NLT)**

There is so much to talk about our homeschooling journey and how much I have learned in the process. Though I had a Master's in Education, I felt completely unequipped to homeschool my children when we started. But I felt called, and Kevin agreed. Though I had grown up in the Baltimore public school system and Kevin had experienced both public and Catholic school, we felt confident that homeschooling our children was the journey our family should take.

Every year, I would pray to God for clear direction...

"Should we homeschool again? If so, should we join a coop? Which one? Which curriculum should I choose for each child for each subject? Was I doing anything wrong? Why could one child read so well while another seemed to struggle? Why did one's handwriting look below level, yet their math skills were light years ahead of their peers? Am I too hard on them? Am I too easy on them? Why, God, why do I second guess every single decision that I'm making on behalf of these children?? Are you sure, like really sure, God, that this is what I'm supposed to be doing????"

One aspect of homeschooling that quickly became a non-negotiable for the Armstrong Academy was Community Bible Study (CBS). Every year, we would register the children and myself. Eventually, I would even become a leader there as well. Doubts about all the homeschool decisions inevitably crept in, but I never once doubted the importance of hiding God's Word in my children's hearts.

CBS was such a blessing to us. I could have time each week in an adult setting, not surrounded by littles that needed me. I could breathe deeply in two hours of peace, discussing God's Word with women of all ages and denominations. It was very much like Paul and Timothy. Paul mentored Timothy and taught Timothy how to mentor others. There were ladies at CBS who were decades farther down in their discipleship walk, and they would gently guide me. And there were others who were newer in their faith, whom I had the privilege of gently guiding. The ladies at CBS taught me over the years how to study God's Word, apply it to whatever situation I endured, and teach it to my children and any other mentees that God placed in my life along the way.

While I would be in my classes, my three children attended classes with other homeschoolers, learning all those "social skills" that many try to claim homeschoolers lack, such as how to raise your hand, ask permission to use the restroom, interact with peers, etc. But more importantly, my children would study the same book of the Bible that I was learning, but in age-appropriate books. Kevin would study the same biblical book at home so that at dinner time or on the weekends, the entire family could discuss the truths each gleaned from God's Word. We all were learning and united as a family in the process.

If I ever had a hard time answering the adult homework questions, I could glance at the kids' books and read them in simpler terms. This helped me break down difficult concepts into bite-sized pieces that were easy to understand. I will admit to doing this multiple times, especially while studying the prophecies in Isaiah and Revelation!

The community aspect of CBS has also proved to be a lifeline repeatedly throughout the years. Having people in my life who cared, were willing to listen, offered advice, and interceded for us in prayer was the greatest gift this young homeschooler could have ever been given. Over the years, I have directed numerous new homeschooling families to CBS simply for the gift of community it offers.

In addition, studying the Bible verse by verse each year proved invaluable in my faith journey. It helped me underline and highlight in the Bibles, which I would end up giving away to others. It hid key truths in my heart, truths about trust, obedience, hardship, prayer, generosity, and so much more that shaped me into the disciple I am today. Nothing can change a person's life like Jesus. And one of the best ways to understand Jesus is to study His Word. CBS kept me in it year after year after year.

Besides CBS, homeschooling taught me that my life was not my own. My life was about serving God and others. Homeschooling taught me to give up on the worldly chaos and seek the things that were most important, such as faith and family. To homeschool, our family indefinitely forfeited a second income, but God always provided. The more I learned about God's sacrificial love for His children, the easier homeschooling seemed to become, for I didn't mind sacrificially loving my family in this way. We learned to live off less and to ultimately be content with what we had.

But let's be 100% honest. Homeschooling had its rough days. You know, the kind where I would turn on a documentary for the kids and go sneak some chocolate in the pantry while their faces were glued to the screen. It also had days where I simply didn't have the physical or mental capacity to teach, and/or the children seemed to have lost their thinking caps. On those days,

I had to remember my MAIN OBJECTIVE in homeschooling - to raise children who grew up to be self-sufficient, educated individuals who loved Jesus and served others. If God could give me grace, I would have to learn to accept it and give it to the children as well.

There were days, I'll admit, that the bookwork was too difficult or time-consuming or too tear-inducing, so we would simply close the books. We would then pray about what it was Jesus would have us do that day. I would encourage the children to think of WHO we could bless in some way, encouraging them to recognize the Holy Spirit's promptings for themselves. A few times in the late spring, when temperatures begin to ridiculously rise in the south, we would go buy a case of water or Gatorade and walk around our neighborhood and find landscapers, roofers, or other construction workers. We would hand out cold drinks as free gifts. Oftentimes, we would come across predominantly Spanish-speaking workers who didn't understand English. That's when we had to quickly Google how to say, "Free, God bless you" in Spanish - "Gratis, Dios te bendiga." In those days, my children learned more about life and love than any book could have taught them. Later, when God would send us to Central America for mission trips, my children were already accustomed to a little of the language and the idea of being Jesus' hands and feet. Today, Ellie is even majoring in Spanish in college. So, what began as a "tough" school day and seemed like a "cop-out" of teaching, God was using as part of His bigger plan for our family!

Other times, especially in the dark, cold month of January, we would wake up each morning asking God to whom we could share some "Son-light." We would purposefully buy oranges, pineapples, yellow daisies or sunflowers, yellow candles, or anything that seemed bright and cheery and bless someone who may have been recovering from the flu or surgery and leave them little splashes of "Son-shine." I thought I was teaching the children to be generous and thoughtful, but it was really God who was moving my heart and teaching me through these experiences to become more generous.

Points to Ponder

1. Though homeschooling is certainly not everyone's calling, we are all still called to direct the children to God. If you are a parent or grandparent, how are you making routine efforts to instill Biblical truths into your children or grandchildren? Even if you are not a parent, are there children God has placed in your life to whom you could direct - nieces/nephews, neighbors, etc.?

2. Have you ever experienced a time when you thought you were helping or teaching someone something, but it was really you who learned in that process? What was it like, and what did you learn?

3. If it's not already part of your daily habit, how could you make daily Bible study part of your routine? What benefits do you think you could gain?

Devotion: What Are You Staring At?

Facebook, November 2023

"What are you staring at??"

I have been thinking about this question a lot lately. And when God gives me something to ponder, it usually ends up as a Facebook devotional. So here you go...

Have you ever been driving in the mountains or a national park, and cars are all pulled over looking down at a particular spot?

- Some will drive by and not give it a second thought.

- Others will drive by and may at least wonder, "What were they looking at?" but continue down the road.

- And then there are those who will stop, wonder what everyone is looking at, and LOOK IN THE SAME DIRECTION. They may even go over to someone and ask, "What are you staring at?" And upon being pointed in the right direction, the ones who pulled over will also get to witness that awesome sight - the mother bear walking with her cute cubs, or that herd of elk running across the valley, or whatever amazing sight that caused everyone to stop and stare.

The point I'm making... Had everyone not been staring, others might not have stopped to look in the same direction.

God pointed this out to me lately when I asked, "How do I show others your love more? God, I'm not great with words, usually putting my foot in my mouth when all I am trying to do is help. But I want others to see YOU."

His answer came to me in the scenario I mentioned above. He told me to simply FOCUS ON HIM.

I should be so transfixed on Him and gazing into His eyes that others wonder what I see as well. And if and when they ask me for details, all I need to do is point out the direction of my gaze—Him. His beauty, His essence, and His presence will do the rest.

Friends, set your eyes upon Christ so intently that others will want to know what it is you see. And when they ask, point them to Jesus, and He can do the rest.

"One thing I ask from the Lord, this only do I seek: that I may dwell in the house of the Lord all the days of my life, to gaze on the beauty of the Lord and to seek him in his temple." Psalms 27:4 (NIV)

"Look to the Lord and his strength; seek his face always." Psalms 105:4 (NIV)

13

Be Brave

"Then I heard the Lord asking, 'Whom should I send as a messenger to this people? Who will go for us?' I said, 'Here I am. Send me.'" Isaiah 6:8 (NLT)

In the fall of 2014 and then in the spring of 2015, God continued to teach me to trust in Him, but He also began to train me to be bold and brave in ways that I had yet to discover.

October is breast cancer awareness month. It's hard to go anywhere without seeing the little pink ribbons everywhere, reminding women of their need for scans. I had never had a mammogram, for I was only in my early thirties. However, my aunt suffered from breast cancer in her early thirties, and an inner voice prompted me to schedule my first mammogram. Because of the family history, thankfully, my insurance was willing to pay for that first mammogram, so I scheduled it.

Unfortunately, that first scan came back abnormal. I was asked to return for another "quick scan." I thought nothing of it, had no fear, no hesitations. It was scheduled for the morning of Ellie's 9th birthday. She had wanted to spend her October birthday at the Billy Graham Library in Charlotte, just a 30-minute drive from our home. So, I took the kids with me to the doctor's office first thing in the morning. They sat quietly together in the waiting room while I went back. After the "quick scan," the radiologist asked to see me in her office. She told me that she *saw something concerning* and was ordering a biopsy.

"*Biopsy? Wasn't that for extracting tissue to check for cancer? You think there's a chance I have cancer??*" I asked the medical professional.

"*We won't know for sure until the biopsy results come back*," she replied.

I was on the verge of tears from the shock, but I had to put on a brave face for my children and get back to them in the waiting room.

We then continued our regularly scheduled birthday field trip. God couldn't have ordained a more perfect plan for our day under these circumstances. We were headed to a place that was infused with volunteers who love Jesus and who are taught to pray with the hurting and afraid. At the completion of the tour, visitors are ushered into the bookstore, where prayer volunteers await. The kids asked to look at the nearby children's book section, and I stood there with a volunteer who prayed with me. I whispered to her about the news I received earlier and asked her to pray fervently that I would be healthy enough to watch my children grow up and celebrate many more birthdays. I don't remember the words that were prayed over me that day, but I remember the sheer peace that flooded over me.

God had a plan for this turn of events. He would give me His peace and a spirit of bravery for whatever came next, and I trusted Him for that.

The following week, Kevin took off work, we dropped the children off at a friend's house, and we went to my biopsy. I was naturally a little nervous but clung to my faith in God's bigger plan.

The technician who prepared me for the biopsy walked in. In my eagerness to not dwell on negative thoughts, I asked her to tell me about herself, and she told me all about her mission work to Nicaragua. I immediately smiled and knew that God had sent me the perfect person at just the time I needed them. I learned that she went on her own to serve the impoverished in Central America. I confessed to her my inner dream of going on mission trips. She told me to simply find a trip and go. The idea had never dawned on me. I always thought I had to go with my church if and whenever they went. It was a foreign concept to me that someone could just decide to go serve in that capacity. This woman may have extracted tissue from me that day to be tested, but she implanted a very important seed in my heart that would grow quicker than any cancer could. Thankfully, my biopsy showed no cancer, but she and I remained in contact.

One day, the following spring, I came across a Facebook post from a neighbor inviting others to attend a mother/daughter retreat at a local camp. I thought a girl's weekend with my 9½-year-old Ellie sounded amazing, so I registered us. Little did I know at the time, but that weekend would change the trajectory of our lives in so many ways.

The theme of the retreat was to "Be Brave." We participated in activities like canoeing on the lake and zip-lining. But it was the small group discussions that really stretched my bravery. Many of the other moms there attended the same church, and some had even gone on mission trips to Guatemala. I happened to make the comment, *"I have always desired to go on a mission trip. I even prayed God would move us to Uganda one day."*

The retreat coordinator told me, *"You and Ellie should come with us to Guatemala next year."*

That little seed my biopsy technician helped plant a few months prior suddenly blossomed. But the fleshy questions quickly followed. *"Could I possibly go with these strangers? Was it crazy to go to a developing country with my daughter? Would Kevin even let me? How could we afford it? Was this part of God's bigger plan???"*

Throughout the weekend, I focused my prayer on handing over those questions and truly seeking God's answers. By the time the weekend was over, I was itching to get home and discuss the possibility with Kevin. I really, really wanted to travel with some of these ladies, do mission work with Ellie, and be the hands and feet of Jesus to the least fortunate.

When we arrived home, tired but joy-filled, I chatted with Kevin. He knew my heart's desire for mission work and agreed that I could take Ellie with this church team the following January. I told him I would teach swim lessons all summer to help cover the costs.

So that's what we did. I taught swim lesson after swim lesson after swim lesson all summer. We paid our deposits and the first few rounds of trip payments.

By the time fall came around, we had fully paid off my trip, but we still owed $700 on Ellie's portion. I had to trust that God would provide. I did all that I could have done, but He would need to do the rest. And He certainly did.

That week at CBS, Ellie's teacher came up to me. Apparently, Ellie had asked for prayer in her class about her trip payments. The teacher wanted to know how much we were short. I told her. She then proceeded to write me a check for that exact amount. I paused her, for she was a young mother as well, and I knew how much of a sacrifice this would be, and I didn't want her to feel obligated. She quickly silenced me and told me about her grandmother, who had recently passed away and who also loved the Lord deeply. In her will, Ellie's teacher received some inheritance money. When she heard Ellie's prayer request, she knew that writing this check would be exactly what her grandmother would want her to do with some of the funds. Being the crybaby that I am, I was instantly in tears. The blessings of a dear saint who was now dancing in Heaven with her Savior would be the catalyst for sending my daughter and me to Guatemala to share the love of Jesus with hurting and impoverished children.

God taught me that He knew the details of everything, and we simply need to trust and obey. I could do all that I could as my act of obedience, but I also needed to trust Him to do the rest. There was this cycle of trust and obedience, this rhythm of life that God was perfecting in my heart. Thankfully, God is so patient.

In January 2016, Ellie and I acted on our bravery as we traveled to Guatemala with a group of practical strangers. We served at a ministry that housed orphans and temporarily displaced children (those whose parents perhaps were in jail or going through counseling to receive custody again). The same day we arrived, three brothers also arrived to stay at this facility. They were scared. Ellie and I were feeling a little out of sorts as well. We both noticed these brothers sitting by themselves as all the other children played games together. Ellie and I approached the boys, who were around 5, 7, and 8 years old. I was missing Ben and Sammy and adjusting to the cultural differences, and these boys looked as if they were lost and confused, too. But God sent us to the same place at the same time. Ellie, who was 10, was a natural big sister and instantly played with the boys. I quickly earned their trust as well and gave them hugs and kisses. We enjoyed the playground together, for there were major language barriers, but play and love are universal.

Later that afternoon, when we visited another area of the ministry where the youngest children stayed, I was drawn to a little toddler hugging a large stuffed gray elephant. He looked so much like Sheila's son Damien, our godson, whom we hadn't seen since moving from Maryland nine years prior. I just wanted to squeeze this little boy and share a motherly hug with him. I would soon learn that he, too, was new to the facility and was the youngest brother of the three boys from the playground.

After a week of serving, it was time to fly home. We had

built houses for the impoverished in a local village, distributed essential food to the hungriest, played lots of futbol with the children, and so much more. It felt incredibly strange to be leaving. Part of me was homesick for my husband and sons. Still, the other part of me knew I would be homesick for this beautiful land and these precious children, especially the four brothers with whom my daughter and I had grown attached. Ellie and I chatted on the flight home about how we just had to return next year and bring Kevin along with us.

Our reunion with Kevin, Ben, and Sammy was sweet. Ellie spoke nonstop about her experience, and I did as well. They found it difficult to understand our experience, for they had never been on a mission trip or immersed in another culture. Ellie began fundraising almost immediately, wanting to raise money to build even more houses for the homeless she met. Her heart had been touched to the core. She and Kevin made an agreement that if she fundraised the money to build more houses, he would go with us the following year on the next trip and help build the houses himself. Both kept their end of the deal. Ellie made coffee candles to sell, gave little speeches to those who would come and listen to her experience, and collected donations. I spent another summer teaching swim lesson after swim lesson.

As the fall came around once again and trip funds were due, I started feeling uneasy about leaving my seven and nine-year-old boys at home while the three of us traveled to Guatemala. Something didn't feel right. Who could I trust to leave the boys with? Sure, we had family and friends who would have taken fine care of them. But my mama's heart was hurting. I realized that I wanted the whole family to travel, not just Kevin, Ellie, and me. But was this what God wanted?? So, I began praying. Then, I started tossing around the idea with Kevin. Funding five family members would be a considerable amount of money, money we didn't really have or plan for. But if God wanted this to happen, He would provide. He had a pattern of providing, right??

After much prayer, Kevin and I both felt the need to take all five of us. We took the leap of faith and paid the deposit for the boys as well. But we would need to come up with an additional $2,000 to pay for their trips quickly. The day after, we bravely signed up the boys, and without telling our family about it, my aunt mailed us a check. And I'm sure you can guess correctly - it was for $2,000. She listened to Ellie and me share our experiences over the last few months. She knew the three of us had been planning to go, and she wanted to help with the costs. She, however, had no idea that we had just sent in the boys' applications and needed that exact amount. God provided yet again. We simply needed to trust and obey.

Traveling with the whole family just felt right. Our children proved to be the perfect ambassadors for our team of adults. Every single one of the children at the Guatemalan ministry had been through abuse or neglect, for that was the reason they were living there. These were traumatized children who rightfully had a hard time trusting adults. By bringing along our own children, the Guatemalan children learned through our children that we were safe and fun to hang out with. We would start by kicking the soccer ball together as a family, and then other children would inevitably want to join in. Our kids played Hot Wheels and marbles with the children there.

Our children learned to serve, paint, and mix concrete by hand, wheelbarrow after wheelbarrow after wheelbarrow full. They used saws, drills, and jackhammers years before we ever would have taught them. They picked up Spanish phrases, tried new foods, and, most importantly, learned compassion. Upon returning, they didn't ask for as much at their birthdays or Christmas, or to eat out. They quickly learned that our spare dollars went to our little friends in Guatemala, sponsoring them when we weren't there or saving so we could visit again.

In November of 2018, we did the bravest thing yet: We went down for an entire month without a team, just the five of us serving. We had already established relationships with the ministry in Guatemala City and another in Chimaltenango. Our plan was to serve at both places.

Planning to be away for a month took incredible faith. We needed to trust God in much more than a week-long short-term mission trip. We needed funds and logistics to pre-pay our bills at home, pet sitters, and so much more. We sacrificed. We prayed. We saved. We fundraised. And God provided, as He always had. There are too many stories of his provision and faithfulness to list. The main point I wish to make is that God had heard our prayers to serve Him on the mission field, and He always provided a way for us to do so.

The closer we seemed to draw near to God, the more we learned about his heart for all his children. Since then, we have taken the children down to Guatemala eight times. Now, at the time of this writing, other foreign mission trips are scheduled with various members of our family to different locations. God heard my prayers years before to be a family on mission. He asked, **"Whom shall I send?"** and we all individually answered, *"Here I am! Send me!"*

Points to Ponder

1. Read *Isaiah 6:8*. If God asked, would you be willing to be a messenger for Him?

2. Have you trusted God with your finances? Would you be willing to invest financially into mission work, whether traveling yourself or helping to send others?

3. Read *Matthew 28:19-20*. As Jesus was preparing to ascend into heaven, he told his disciples in verse 19 to go and make disciples, but what does He also promise in verse 20? Do you believe in that promise?

Devotion: Part of an Essay Ellie Wrote About Guatemala
Circa February 2019 (She was 13 at the time)

"Questions.
As I sit here and write, I try to reconcile my two worlds. One world where people dress to impress, are kept to a tight schedule, always in a rush, and ignore the people around them. The other where people don't care what you wear, where time is fluid, and you never rush, always take your time, and always see the people around you who need help.

It's like fitting a square into a circle hole. It doesn't fit. You have to be willing to give up one or the other. You can't have both. You need to pick, or nothing will ever make sense. You can join the world and fit in, find the acceptance of others, but lose the love and peace, or you can go against the flow, against everything ingrained in you and lose the acceptance of others, be an outcast, but gain everything that's actually worthwhile.

You have to decide how much you're actually willing to give up to live out your calling. Are you willing to give up your calling and a life of vibrancy and fulfillment for a life of social acceptance that will fluctuate with the winds? Or do you stick with your calling and face the judgment of your peers, of the criticism of the world, the harsh words and angry stares? You have to decide who and what is worth more. Your peers and their acceptance, or Jesus and his eternal life and crown of glory?

There are pros and cons to each, but it is a personal choice. Which will you choose?"

14

Two-sided Missions

"So let's do it—full of belief, confident that we're presentable inside and out. Let's keep a firm grip on the promises that keep us going. He always keeps his word. Let's see how inventive we can be in encouraging love and helping out... spurring each other on..." Hebrews 10:22-25 (MSG)

One interesting thing about fundraising for all our trips to Guatemala was that they involved me teaching swim lessons in my neighborhood during the summers. I didn't initially realize it, but God was sending me on mission in my "Uganda" so that I could go serve as a missionary in Central America. Teaching one-on-one swim lessons bonds an instructor and student if done correctly. There is a lot of trust-building while incorporating skill and fun. My favorite lessons are the ones where I can take a child who is afraid of the water and eventually help them discover the new, wonderful world that exists underwater.

I once had a little girl who was deathly afraid of the water, and I mean deathly afraid of even drops of water on her face. I patiently worked with her, and she was swimming by the end of the summer. That autumn, her mother texted me about her getting her getting baptized. She said, *"What you taught my daughter in the swimming pool is having eternal blessings. She got baptized today. Thank you so much!"*

Oftentimes, we have a heart's desire, but God doesn't always send us on the most direct route or answer our prayers right away. Abraham and Sarah, for instance, had to wait 25 years for Isaac to be born so that they had time to learn to rely on God. Joseph had to spend years away from his family, some years even in jail, learning how to wait on God and forgive his brothers. The Israelites had to wander in the desert for 40 years to learn to trust God before their nation was able to enter the Promised Land. And sometimes, God doesn't answer the prayers the way we envisioned them. David prayed to build God a house, but God told him it would be his son, Solomon, who would build the temple.

I had to wait to become a mother first, and then, later, a missionary. God needed me to learn very important truths first. It was essential that God become first in my marriage so that we could then parent biblically. And I still have never been to Uganda. God had to teach me the true definition of a 'missionary' first— **one who serves a missional purpose.**

God may or may not ever choose to send me to Africa; oddly enough, I'm ok with that. But I'm also positive that He gave me the desire to serve others and then expected me to use that desire wherever He placed me. Every summer between our Guatemala trips, I taught swim lessons in our neighborhood. Initially, I simply saw it as a way to earn the finances to fund airline tickets. But God quickly showed me that my summers were my missional training sessions. He was allowing me to work with children, build their trust, show them unconditional love, and teach them life skills. These are all skill sets that I needed on the Guatemalan mission field that I learned in South Carolina pool water.

Because I'm so extroverted, I loved spending time with not just my swim students but their families as well. If I were ever at the pool outside of lessons, I could easily be found playing sharks and minnows or marco polo with my former students and their siblings. Or I might be sitting on the side of the pool, lending a listening ear to a stressed mama. I would hold babies while parents needed to rush potty-trained children to the restroom. I would offer band-aids and Benadryl for little-skinned knees or bee stings. And on more than a dozen occasions thus far, God has placed me at just the right spot at just the right moment to rescue drowning children.

Having lifeguarded in college, I have been trained on how to spot a distressed swimmer and to quickly rescue them. I also learned how to watch the at-risk children more closely - those who might be with a busy parent who gets distracted by one child but then turns their back on a toddler for but a second. Our community pool doesn't fund lifeguards, unfortunately, but once a lifeguard, always a lifeguard. I couldn't help but watch the children at our pool every time I was there.

I never could have imagined all that God was planning by having me teach lessons. By meeting so many families in our community, I also began pet-sitting for many of my swim families throughout the whole year. By doing this, I was earning a little more income during the off-season as well, equaling more funds saved for mission trips and more opportunities to get to know my neighbors. I never marketed these jobs, but they came to me by word of mouth. God was pouring out his blessings on us right here. I have never really calculated all that I have earned through swim lessons and pet sitting, but I know for a fact that it far exceeds the initial $1,000 God asked me to anonymously give to my neighbors that first night I asked to become a missionary.

The spiritual blessings far exceed the financial ones. I have spent time praying with many neighbors, inviting them to church, hosting Bible studies, or simply gaining more neighborly Facebook friends who would then be exposed to the numerous devotions I post. God is more imaginative than we could ever give Him credit for. He is also way more faithful.

God would soon teach me that becoming an organ donor could also be qualified as mission work as well.

Points to Ponder

1. When you are asked to wait on God to answer your prayers, do you see the time of waiting as also an important time of learning?

2. Read the Hebrews passage at the beginning of this chapter, how could you be encouraging others? Is there a certain person God is laying on your heart who needs to be reminded that God always keeps his promises?

Devotion: The Beauty of the Son-Light

Facebook, December 2022

"Moses came down from Mount Sinai, carrying the Ten Commandments. His face was shining brightly because the Lord had been speaking to him. But Moses did not know at first that his face was shining." Exodus 34:29 (CEV)

I've been studying Exodus the last few months and keep thinking of this passage and how it reminds me of a good summer tan...

Is your face radiating and shining from spending time with God?

I know in the summers when I'm in the sun six days a week teaching swim lessons, it shows on my face. My skin tans and one can see the marks around my eyes from my sunglasses, from being in the sun so much.

But as winter approaches and I'm inside much more, my tan fades, and I become much paler.

Sometimes, I think spending time with God is like a tan. The more you spend time in prayer and reading His Word, the more it shows on your face, in how it shines and radiates - just like Moses experienced.

Just because it's wintertime, don't become too 'pale.' Instead, soak up the SON! (It is HIS birthday season, after all...)

And the beauty of Son-light, it never burns! You can never get too much of it...

GAME TIME: Learning to Obey

Devotion: Bible Reading Challenge

Facebook, December 2019

I did it!! This goal-oriented girl decided last year to read through my NIV study Bible in 2019, and to journal along the way in my Memory Journal. I wanted to be able to give Ellie my study Bible, with all my notes and highlighting and to challenge her in 2020 to read it as well. And my Memory Journal - aka the Cliff Notes - is for the boys to read, as an introduction to getting them into this same habit.

The kids and I have participated in Community Bible Study for the last 11 1/2 years (since Ben was an infant). Each year, we intensely study a book (or a few books) of the Bible. But I had never made the effort to read it from cover to cover until my buddy and prayer partner challenged me. (Everyone needs a buddy like this in their lives!)

Jesus is everywhere in the Bible, not just the New Testament.

God's love for YOU is on every single page.

I challenge YOU to begin this journey, too. My gifts to my kids this Christmas are not just the Bible and journal, but the Example, that every morning when they would wake up, they knew where they would find me and what I would be doing. (It also meant that I had to move my workouts to the predawn hours to squeeze everything into my days).

I am not sure how many gallons of coffee I have consumed, but this is the gift that will keep on giving in my life, the life of my marriage, my parenting, and the lives of future generations of Armstrongs and those with whom we come in contact.

"I have hidden your word in my heart that I might not sin against you." Psalms 119:11 (NIV)

15

The Calling

"And don't forget to do good and to share with those in need..."
Hebrews 13:16 (NLT)

Donating part of myself always seemed so natural. When I was 16, I started donating blood in the Red Cross drives hosted in my high school cafeteria. Over the next 20 years, I would donate whenever I could fit it into my schedule, had high enough iron, wasn't pregnant, hadn't traveled overseas recently, etc. If I was eligible, I would always try. It just became part of my routine. Because of this habit, I learned that I had AB+ blood, one of the rarest types, with only 3-4% of the American population having it.

I still remember that one of my first thoughts on 9/11, when I could see the smoke from the Pentagon from my office building, was, "I need to go donate in case they need my blood type." God had planted the seed early in my mind that part of my body could help save someone's life. Nowadays, I even joke, saying, "Blood donation is often the gateway drug to organ donation."

I still remember where I was when God first asked. I was sitting in my living room one evening in early December 2019. I don't remember what the rest of the family was doing, but I was scrolling Facebook. In that process, I came across a news article that captured my heart. It was about a local six-year-old boy who had my rare blood type and needed a kidney. That mindless social media scrolling would end up being a divine catalyst.

Instantly, as I read about the little boy's story, my heart went out to his mother. I didn't know her or her son, but I knew all about a mother's love for her child. I also had experience with fear, anxiety, and loss. When Ellie was nine months old, her pediatrician told us there was a possibility she had hydrocephalus or a brain tumor due to her abnormal head circumference growth rates. We needed an MRI to determine that she was fine. But the time between the 'possibility' of a serious condition and the relief of realizing it was nothing was agonizing. When Ben was four weeks old, he spiked a fever so high that he was admitted to the hospital and needed a spinal tap. He had difficulty breathing, and I was forbidden from holding him (and sharing my body heat) until the fever came down for fear of a seizure. All throughout his toddlerhood, we dealt with respiratory infections that required round-the-clock nebulizer treatments and more. When he was ten, he was hospitalized again for his asthmatic issues related to respiratory infections. When Sammy was around seven, he had a scary tooth infection that required IV antibiotics, and just a few years later, a serious parasitic infection landed him a few days in the hospital as well, just days after we returned from our month-long trip to Guatemala. And, of course, my children have had their share of stitches, staples, broken bones, bonded teeth, viral infections, stomach bugs, and more. Every injury or illness hurts a mama's heart.

So, it was the mama of this little AB+ kidney-needing boy that my heart went out to. I couldn't help but think, "If it were my child who was this seriously ill, I would want someone to step up and help them."

Without even discussing it with Kevin, I instantly clicked the link on that Facebook page and filled out my information in the event his case worker wanted to contact me and have me tested. Then I waited. And prayed. And waited some more. And prayed a lot more.

A few weeks later, I contacted the coordinator and was told that there had been such an overwhelming response to that social media campaign that they had many others whom they were testing first. They would let me know if they needed me. I never heard from that coordinator again.

But the seed in my heart had been planted. I went ahead and filled out a preliminary online questionnaire with the Donor Care Network, not really expecting it would amount to anything.

As 2020 began, I received an email asking me to fill out a complete medical history questionnaire to continue my registration into the Network. I was hesitant about this. But that same week, my Bible study leader challenged me to pray about a Word of the Year. What one word was God giving me for this year? As I prayed about it, I felt the word was "**Help**."

Romans 10:13 MSG says, *"Everyone who calls, 'Help, God!' gets help."*

Give help. Get help. Be the help.

I didn't know what God was doing, but He was preparing my heart to **help** in some manner.

For the first week of January, I couldn't shake the idea of donation. I was consumed with it. I did multiple online searches to learn more. I learned about how long most people wait on the transplant list, 3-5 years. YEARS! I also learned that about 13 people a day die while waiting for a kidney donor. 13 die every day! 13 souls who might not know Jesus!

These numbers burdened me, and I didn't know anyone personally on the list.

"What if my child was on the list?" I thought.

Then God spoke to my heart in the only way He can, "**Everyone is somebody's child.**"

"God, are you asking me what I think you are asking me? Just donate to whomever??"

"Yes. Trust me."

"Father, if you want me to donate, you are going to have to work on Kevin's heart, too."

Up until now, I hadn't mentioned any of this to Kevin yet. I had been researching and praying, but quietly for a few weeks.

Then, we went out on a special date night together. I prayed beforehand and knew that this evening would be the perfect time to disclose to Kevin what God was laying on my heart. I was so nervous that night! On January 11th, we went out to dinner. We stayed at the restaurant for hours, talking and enjoying each other's company. Kevin had questions about kidney donation, but being the faith-filled man that he is, he was supportive of me following God's call.

At that point, I had no idea why God was sending me down this path. As I told Kevin that night, *"Maybe God just wants me to go through all the required medical testing because He wants me to discover something about my body that needs attention. I have read stories of potential donors finding cancers or diseases that they didn't know they had, and had they not gone through the process, they wouldn't have found out before it was too late."*

We didn't know if the final destination would be an operating room, but we agreed that we were willing to take the next step on this path. From that night forward, we began praying together about this new journey. I then registered with the National Kidney Registry to begin the process of becoming a non-designated living donor. With Kevin's support, I had my answer to God's tough question about being willing to donate to anyone.

Yes, I would be willing to give to whomever God matched me with, even if I never even learned who they were.

Kevin and I trusted that God had a plan, even if we couldn't envision all the details. We prayed that if God truly wanted me to donate, every door would be opened.

Throughout that time, I kept remembering my favorite poem from high school, "Not in Vain" by Emily Dickinson.

God had been planting the seed of helping others decades before He ever called me to it...

If I can stop one heart from breaking,
I shall not live in vain.
If I can ease one life the aching,
Or cool one pain,
Or help one fainting robin
Unto his nest again,
I shall not live in vain.

Points to Ponder

1. What is the biggest thing God has ever asked of you? How did you respond?

2. Have you ever been afraid of sharing your deepest conversations with God with others? If so, why? What were you afraid of? If you ended up sharing those conversations, how did that go?

3. No matter the month that you may be reading this in, what is the Word of the Year you think God might be asking you to focus on? Which Scripture passages can you read and study to help you maintain that focus?

4. Sometimes, God asks us to just "take the next step" in a faith journey, not knowing the final destination He is planning. Is God currently asking you to simply "take the next step" in anything right now? If so, how are you responding?

Devotion: Listen to the Word

Facebook, June 2022

I didn't sleep well last night. I woke up a few times and finally, I set my alarm for an hour later and turned on my Bible app to the audio setting. I thought I would listen to some Ephesians and Philippians while I either tried to get up or fall back asleep for a little bit more. Apparently, I fell asleep and had this dream...

I was a teenager back in the public-school setting, but my dream set in the modern day since I had a phone (I didn't get a phone till college – yeah, I'm that old). In my dream, the teacher was trying to lecture, but my phone kept preaching the Message. My teacher asked me to turn off the Bible. I tried to hit the pause button, but it wouldn't stop. I tried closing the app, but it would not stop. I tried asking tech-savvy friends for help, but nothing they did could get it to stop. The teacher suggested I turn off the phone completely, which I attempted, and it still would not stop. I was told to put it in the hallway, but it would not stop, and others brought it back in and said it was bothering them. I was apologizing and panicking because I felt out of control.

No matter how hard I tried, no matter what I did, no matter what experts or those in authority attempted to silence the Message, it continued to broadcast.

Then, my alarm went off. I woke up and hit the pause button. It finally stopped.

This dream really got me thinking. You see, I wasn't in the right 'dimension' to have any power to turn off my phone in my dream. We humans think we know what's best. We think we can turn God on and off whenever we like. But He exists outside of our realm because He is bigger than it all and the creator of the world in which we live in. His Message will be proclaimed regardless of our actions.

Maybe it's time we started listening to the Words instead of trying to fruitlessly shut them off. We'd find peace instead of panic. We'd find love instead of hate. We'd find truth instead of lies.

We need to Start listening. We need to Spend more time listening instead of using all our energy trying to turn it off. The Word is everywhere if we are just willing to listen.

Point to ponder for today.

16

The Process - "The First Trimester"

"Trust in the Lord with all your heart and lean not on your own understanding; in all your ways submit to him, and he will make your paths straight." Proverbs 3:5-6 NIV

No one could have predicted all that 2020 would unleash. I never imagined the entire pre-donation process would take nine months. What could normally take just a few short weeks was stretched out drastically due to a new virus that would wreak havoc worldwide that year. But God always has a plan, and I trusted in that. In God's ultimate nudging, I kept a detailed journal for the first time in my life.

The beginning of this donation process could be compared to when a woman first learns that she is pregnant. The early stages can be full of all sorts of emotions: fear, joy, uncertainty, and more. But there is the realization that life is about to change and never be the same again. A seed has been planted, and growth has begun.

By January 20, 2020, two weeks after I shared with Kevin my heart and we agreed together to proceed, I had filled out another online medical questionnaire and was thus sent a urine sample kit. If you have never collected a 24-hour urine sample, it is a unique experience. You are sent a large golden plastic container and are asked to collect all urine for one entire day. You must clear your schedule or plan to carry the container and a cooler with ice with you everywhere you go. Thankfully, I was able to stay at home and keep mine in my refrigerator that day.

After a day's worth of urine was collected, I drove my container thirty minutes to the closest lab and had my first blood drawn. I would make this drive multiple times throughout the upcoming months, every time a new urine or blood sample was needed for me to jump over the next hurdle in the donation process.

A few days later, our family returned to Guatemala for another two-week mission trip in late January and early February. I remember sitting with our Guatemalan pastor friend in Chimaltenango and telling her how God was nudging me toward donating a kidney. She promised to pray for me and even took me to visit a local mother who needed a kidney. Since we had different blood types and that Guatemalan kidney transplants are incredibly rare, I knew God wasn't planning for me to donate directly to this woman. However, that visit to her home was an eye-opening experience where I first observed the struggles of someone with kidney disease. I learned how her children were distressed about their mother's health condition, how her husband worried for her, and how taxing dialysis treatments were for patients and their entire families. While in Guatemala on that trip, God kept repeating *Isaiah 41:10 NIV* to my heart...

"So do not fear, for I am with you; do not be dismayed, for I am your God. I will strengthen you and help you; I will uphold you with my righteous right hand."

There was that word, **HELP**, again. A week after we returned to the States, I found myself in a boot from a stress fracture to my foot. I had to withdraw from my half marathon for which I had been training. Injuries like that are disappointing to runners, especially with a race a few weeks away, but I chose to focus on this new "mission" to which God had called me.

In addition, Kevin, Sammy, and Ben all contracted respiratory infections, having picked up an unknown illness on the international flight home. Kevin and Ben seemed to heal within two weeks, but Sammy was left in a miserable state. He had a nasty cough that lasted for months.

On February 18th, I chose my transplant center: Emory in Atlanta, Georgia. It was only a four-hour drive from our home. Additionally, Emory was a reputable National Kidney Registry (NKR) facility that performed hundreds of transplant surgeries a year. Kevin and I both felt more comfortable with my donation taking place there as opposed to a facility that may have been geographically closer to home, but with the tradeoff of less experience.

On March 3rd, I returned to the podiatrist and was told that I had to continue wearing the boot for another three weeks. God was teaching me patience and reliance on Him. In addition, I was learning to listen to that still, small voice everywhere I went and the joy that comes from being used by Him. In my journal that day, I wrote....

As I was checking out, the lady in front of me was checking out first. She was around 60 years old and also in a boot. The office manager told her that she still had a balance of $149 on her account. The injured patient said, "*I can pay $10 toward it*," as she handed the office manager a $10 bill. The manager gave her a receipt, clearly showing her that she still had a balance of well over $100.

I felt such a Holy Spirit compassion toward this woman whom I had never met and most likely would never meet.

God was nudging my heart, *"Wouldn't it be nice to pay off this lady's bill for her?"*

I looked in my wallet and only found $20. But God wasn't telling me to pay towards this lady's bill. He was telling me to pay it off.

Now, I have generously given to strangers before, paying for their groceries or coffee, but this still felt different.

As I was praying in my head about what God wanted me to do, suddenly, the lady was done and leaving the doctor's office.

I felt like I had missed my opportunity.

I stepped up to pay my $20 copay when the office manager said, *"No worries. It looks like you have a credit on your account."*

Confused, I asked, *"What? How?"*

"Apparently, your insurance covered the cost of your boot that you paid for a few weeks ago."

Instantly, I asked, *"Well, how much is the credit?"*

"$225."

I knew then what I was supposed to do. I told the manager that I would like to apply my credit to the balance of the patient before me.

A look of total shock came across the manager's face, "Really??"

"Absolutely! The insurance company blessed me and not everyone has that gift."

So, we worked it out. My fellow boot wearer was blessed with a paid-off bill. I didn't have a copay and still walked away with a $70 credit to my account.

On the drive home from the podiatrist, the office manager called me. "Mrs. Armstrong, I want you to know that I called the other patient for whose bill you paid off. She was moved to tears and asked me to call you and tell you, 'That you don't know how much God used you today.'"

I, of course, was then moved to tears. God had answered her prayers. She paid all that she could, and God did the rest. And we are both glorifying Him today. All because I realized the nudging of the Holy Spirit and listened and obeyed. How lovely it is to be used by God! My prayer is for that lady, whose name I don't even know. I pray all her other financial worries are handled by God, too. And may she pass on the gift of generosity whenever she can. May the doctor's staff be blessed by witnessing it. May my children be blessed by my sobbing tears as I retold them the story.

And may I remember to count it all joy when I face trials of various kinds. If I have to pay money for a boot that I am forced to wear for 8 weeks just for God's glory to be shown in this lady's life, the podiatrist's office, or anyone else who hears this story, then yes - it is joyful, and oh so worth it!

In my journal for March 6, I wrote how excited I was that I had met the minimum requirements to proceed with an evaluation to be a nondirected donor at Emory. I then arranged appointments for my physical with my general practitioner, my mammogram at the local Radiology Center, and the "full workup" to be done on April 1st and 2nd in Atlanta. The latter would have involved a CT scan, EKG, ultrasound, and meeting with the social worker, surgeon, nephrologist, transplant coordinator, and financial coordinator, all in one day of back-to-back appointments. I also first learned about the family voucher program, something I had never heard about until then. When an altruistic donor like me donates to the National Kidney Registry with no intended recipient, they are then issued vouchers for up to 5 family members. In the event one of those 5 needs a kidney in the future, they could "cash in" their voucher for an elevated position on the kidney transplant list. This knowledge was a gift to me, for it took away any possible worries that I should "reserve" my donation "just in case one of my children needed a kidney in the future." As Ephesians 2:10 states, God was preparing in advance for me to do this good work. He was gifting me with answers to questions or concerns I hadn't even thought of yet.

In addition, I journaled at this time about praying over the upcoming school year for my children. Some years, we had participated in homeschool cooperatives, where I would teach a course to other homeschoolers and my children would have opportunities to take classes from other homeschool moms. In early March, I wrote how God was clearly telling me *not* to sign up for the fall, to simply take the next year and homeschool at home. I didn't realize it then in early March of 2020, but our family wouldn't have been able to maintain the commitments of a cooperative the following school year. Again, God knew the future, and I certainly didn't, but He was making our paths straight. All we needed to do was trust Him an take obedient steps in the direction He guided.

All my necessary appointments for donating were finally scheduled, and everything seemed to be advancing quite rapidly. I simply said *"yes"* to every door God opened.

But then came COVID, quarantine, and the cancellation of EVERYTHING. On March 13th, I wrote, *"The world as we have known it is temporarily on hold."*

My heart ached for every single person on the transplant waiting list. Because I was invested in this process and slowly learning more and more about kidney disease, I realized the devastation the quarantine was doing for everyone who wasn't sick with COVID. It was canceling transplant surgeries and creating a backlog of appointments for others waiting for healing. I already knew that people died every day waiting for new kidneys, but COVID cancellations meant even more would die. I also feared for those who were sick with kidney disease and what COVID could do to them.

I began to earnestly pray for my recipient and all others who might be losing hope. I prayed that Isaiah 41:10 verse again, that they would not fear, but instead trust that God would strengthen them and to be reassured that He was sending **HELP**.

All the while, my youngest still could not get over his cough. We were thankfully able to get him into the pediatrician on March 13th due to his chest pains and shortness of breath. Our recent international travel was a blessing in the sense that he qualified for one of the rare early COVID tests. Thankfully, he tested negative, and chest x-rays showed no pneumonia, but his cough kept us already social distancing from crowds for the last month in hopes that we wouldn't share germs with anyone. God was protecting us (and my kidney I hoped to donate) at the same time from potential cases of COVID.

With COVID taking over the world and the cancellations, I wrote on March 18th...

"I'm not sure how my kidney donation falls into all this. It may get postponed if we need to shelter in place and I can't get to Atlanta April 1st. But God is in control always. And with knowing that one thing, I have peace."

And on March 25th....

"Life keeps changing, not even daily but hourly. New laws. New restrictions. New diagnoses. New deaths. New everything. Thank you, God, that You never change. *Hebrews 13:8 says that 'Jesus Christ is the same yesterday, today, and forever.'*"

I'll be honest; it seems that there is a spiritual battle always raging around us, one that is invisible to the naked eye but can be felt. Whenever a believer tries to align themself with the will of God, the evil powers of this world are not happy.

On April 1st, my original plan was to be at Emory having a full workup done, which would clear me to be placed on the National Kidney Registry. It, of course, was postponed with all the initial COVID cancellations. But that night, the spiritual oppression of anxiety tried to creep back into my mind after having been kicked out years prior. I journaled....

"I had a nightmare last night - as if there was demonic oppression going on. I kicked and screamed for Satan to leave, and I shouted out the name of Jesus. Kev woke me up from my sleep and prayed with me. I didn't get much more sleep after that. But as soon as I got out of bed, I saw the most beautiful sunrise. A new day! I read *Isaiah 60:1 NIV, "Arise, shine, for your light has come, and the glory of the Lord rises upon you."* This verse was so beautiful. I anointed all the door frames, windowpanes, and bedposts with oil as I prayed for protection around my family and our home... May my anxieties calm down. May God's name be higher than anything. May God's love be evident everywhere."

At this stage of the donation process, like the end of a woman's first trimester of pregnancy, my heart began to connect to another life, my recipient's. I did not know anything about them, but I had love and concern for their well-being. I began wondering about them - who they were, what they were like, were they ok, what was their future going to be like, and so much more. They didn't have a name or gender yet in my mind, but God had divinely implanted a love for them within my heart, and it was growing. Oh, was it growing!

Points to Ponder

1. Concentrate on the truths in **Ephesians 2:10**. Do you truly believe that God has prepared for you to do good works? If so, is He nudging you in a certain direction?

2. Read **Proverbs 3:5-6** in a few different versions. What is it that God wants you to trust Him about? How can you further develop that intimate trust with Him?

3. Read **Isaiah 60:1** and thank God for this day. Dedicate it to Him. Seek His perfect will for you today.

Devotion: A New Routine
From Holly's Journal, April 2020

"The realization that life won't return to normal in a while has set in. But what was normal? Do we even want to go back to that?

Each season is different somehow. There are seasons of warmth and sunshine, seasons of cold, rainy days, seasons of busy sports schedules, and seasons of lazy days at the pool. We are having to redefine how we live and make a new normal. Life might even change again soon.

I'm realizing that I just hold onto routine too much - and with God, routine means I'm in control and not Him.

I need to get back into the routine of simply arising each day and thanking God for the beautiful day He has given me - the birds chirping, the sun shining, the ability to breathe and to walk, and a family to be with.

God is my guide, not my ride. I can't tell Him where to go, but He shows me.

"Trust in the Lord with all your heart; do not depend on your own understanding. Seek his will in all you do, and he will show you which path to take." Proverbs 3:5-6 NLT

18

The Process - "The Second Trimester"

"Before I formed you in the womb I knew you, before you were born I set you apart; I appointed you as a prophet to the nations." "Alas, Sovereign Lord," I said, "I do not know how to speak; I am too young." But the Lord said to me, "Do not say, 'I am too young.' You must go to everyone I send you to and say whatever I command you. Do not be afraid of them, for I am with you and will rescue you," declares the Lord."
Jeremiah 1:5-8 NIV

My "second trimester" was full of asking inward questions to myself...

- *Why would I donate something like this, especially when I didn't have a family member or close friend in dire need of a kidney?*
- *Why would I just voluntarily give my kidney?*
- *Why subject my healthy body to unnecessary surgery?*
- *Why would I be willing to give up all my sports, activities, exercise classes, running my miles, walking my dogs, swimming laps, and coaching volleyball games - all which I love so dearly and daily participate in one form or another - to give them up for at least two months*

of recovery?
- Why the risk?
- Why, why, why???

Every time, I took my questions to God. He kept reassuring me to trust Him. Thankfully, besides a few trusted Bible study friends and prayer buddies, we kept this kidney donation process to ourselves. All the questions I was asking myself were enough. I didn't want other people placing unnecessary doubts in my mind as well. Kevin and I felt very confident in the path that God was sending us; I did not want to invite others into my mental space. I was afraid some might mean well but be the source of doubts. I refused to give Satan that foothold.

In **Matthew 16**, we learn about how Jesus was predicting his death to his disciples. Peter meant well when he took his Savior aside and rebuked Him, saying, ***"Never, Lord! This shall never happen to you!"***

In verse 23, Jesus turned and said to Peter, ***"Get behind me, Satan! You are a stumbling block to me; you do not have in mind the concerns of God, but merely human concerns."***

This was where I was mentally and spiritually in that "second trimester." I did not want others with good intentions to speak mere "human concerns" to me. I could do that just fine within my own head! I only wanted those who would encourage me to continue to focus on the concerns of God.

In late May, I received a phone call that appointments were slowly opening back up as COVID cases started to decline. May 31st, I wrote…...

"My prayer is still, Lord, Here I am. Send me. If this is my mission field for this time, then so be it. My body is God's body given to me. If God does not want me to donate, then He can put some roadblocks ahead of me. I will follow His lead. But I also pray for the individual who is crying out to God right now, wanting a miracle, needing a donor.

May you, Lord, sustain them with faith in You and hope that you are still working. I wrote on 2/6/20, *"Now then, whatever God has said to you, do." Genesis 31:16.* I will continue with this. Lord, direct my paths, please. Open and close the doors you want to guide me through."

On June 1st, I had a Zoom call with all those doctors and coordinators I was supposed to meet with in person on April 1st. We discussed my motivation for donating, my family history, my home life, my medical history, and everything, including my sanity, with the psychologist. As I told them when they asked me, "Why are you donating?" I would tell them that as my love for God has deepened over time, my love for others has as well. I told them about our mission work and how I first prayed, *"Here I am, Lord, send me"* all those years ago. I told them that I had been given a brave, bold, and fearless spirit. When God called me back to Guatemala all those different times, I obeyed. When God called me to feed the homeless or donate funds to various organizations, or make my neighbors a meal, I obeyed.

And I realized that every single time, I was always blessed by those acts of obedience. Would it be different when the stakes are higher? God teaches his followers to trust and obey. He doesn't say to only trust Him in the easy decisions, like should I take the neighbor a casserole? He simply commands trust and obey. Period. It does take a little more confidence to comply when agreeing to unnecessary major surgery for a complete stranger, but my heart, mind and spirit knew it really was the same.

That second trimester, I knew that my recipient was a child of God's. He/she was created in HIS image. I know that God had a special plan for their life. And perhaps my kidney was part of that plan. Perhaps even they may have needed to be shown a sacrificial act of love, like a stranger sharing their organ with them for physical healing, to finally fully grasp the intensity of God's sacrificial act of love for them by sending Jesus for their spiritual healing. Who can fathom all the mysteries of God??? But I became so excited to be trusted enough to be given a glimpse of His plan, a piece of the puzzle. As a volleyball player and coach, I wanted to be "sent into the game and off of the bench." I kept praying...

"Here I am. Send me. I want in this game! I can HELP. I am willing to play, and I want to do all that I can while I have the time."

God was so faithful to send me little notes of encouragement throughout the process. On June 4th, I wrote...

"God gave me the blessing of hearing a sermon about generosity. The pastor talks about giving a kidney! He knew a man who had donated a kidney and "it was the best thing" he thought he ever did. It was just so sweet to hear to know that God hears me. I don't really have too many reservations, yet, about this. It's still so far out in the future. But the confirmation through the sermon was beautiful to my ears. Yes, I'm giving to be generous. Yes, I'm not the only 'crazy' one out there. Yes, those who have gone before me don't regret it, and still consider it a blessing - to themselves even!"

In the middle of June, I was able to get in with a new general practitioner. The one I had been to in the past didn't have the capability to do an EKG and chest X-ray at their office, and I needed both as the next hurdles to jump in this process. I wrote about this appointment in my journal...

"The doctor looked to be of Indian descent, so I

automatically assumed she was not a Christian. That was so terrible of me. So, when she asked me why I was donating a kidney to a stranger, I had a choice:

1.   Give her an indirect answer that I would want someone to step up if it were my family in need, which technically is still true, or

2.   Give the full truth, the missional answer, the "God gets the glory" answer, but this is sometimes hard for non-Christians to understand without assuming that I am certifiably insane - "God told me to."

In my weakness, I went with both, but I at least led off with God getting the glory. The day I made this appointment, I had been praying that every step I took toward the operating room was on God's perfect path—if not, please put up a roadblock. More importantly, I began praying for everyone who would be touched and inspired by this story. So, in answer to that, God sent me this new doctor at an 11:20 a.m. appointment on June 16th.

When I told her that "God told me to donate" and I was there out of an act of obedience to Him, she replied, "I have chills," as she looked at the hair standing on her arms. She had felt God. That brought me so much joy. And at the end of the appointment, when she asked me "one last question," - it wasn't about my health history or the EKG, but instead it was, "What church do you go to?" I was able to then have a deeper conversation and learned that she was not only a new believer but was new to the area, and she had just started attending the same church where my CBS was held...Thank you, God, for sending me to that doctor's office. I pray for her that she gets connected and grows deeply in her faith...I pray she finds the community she needs and becomes part of a group that will encourage her to dig deep into Your Word. Surround her with patient, loving disciples."

Kevin and I created the phrase "Go B.I.G." a few years ago. It stands for "Be Intentionally Generous." We always wanted to instill this character trait in our children. Generosity isn't something that comes naturally to the world, but it does to God. We wanted our children to always be looking for ways to Go B.I.G.! I never imagined how BIG I would be asked to go!

June 21st, I had been studying *2 Corinthians 8* in my quiet time: *"Now finish the work, so that your eager willingness to do it may be matched by your completion of it...At the present time your plenty will supply what they need..." (vs. 11, 14a)* I wrote....

"Go B.I.G. 2020. Be Intentionally Generous! I have two very well-functioning kidneys, while others may not even have one functioning properly. God gave me this desire to donate. He is now giving me the command "to finish the work." I am to become poor like Jesus did so another can become rich. I pray for everyone who hears the story of my recipient, the story of my "Why?" that they may fall to their knees in thankfulness and glory to our Lord Jesus Christ, who led by example and who inspires, saves, redeems, and wants us to have 'equality' with Him, as a child of God with an admission ticket into Heaven. *2 Corinthians 9:13 NIV says, "Because of the service by which you have proved yourselves, others will praise God for the obedience that accompanies your confession of the gospel of Christ, and for your generosity in sharing with..."*

On Father's Day that year, we had a backyard barbeque with some neighbors. That evening, after talking with some friends, I journaled. I wrote....

"Toward the end, we were talking about my kidney donation, and (a friend) called it an anointing. Even as a pastor,
he said that he wasn't sure he could do that. I feel it is Spir-
it-driven. Most do not understand. Most men do not agree
with Kevin for going along with it. But when (a neighbor)
asked me, "Why?" I simply answered, "God told me to." She
was like, "Ok, I can't argue with that!" When God speaks,
we must obey. When God says go - we must go."

God truly spent the middle months of this donation process teaching me just how a newly pregnant mother might have so
much to learn about motherhood. I had so much to learn about
donating, but even more to learn about God's purposes for me and
about obeying his commands. He patiently taught me every step of
the way. On June 24th, I journaled all that I had been learning....

"God formed me with a **purpose**. He set me apart for a
purpose. He gave me AB+ blood, a healthy kidney, and
the spiritual gift of generosity for a **purpose**. I must go and
do whatever He commands, and go do it without fear, but
with confidence because I am SENT...

A person cannot approach a king, judge, or president on
his own. He must be summoned by them or approached
with confidence when one who has greater authority has
sent them.

My kids may not feel comfortable knocking on a neighbor's or even a stranger's door to ask for a cup of sugar, but
if I send them, they will receive an added boost of encouragement, confidence, and a sense of purpose to complete
the task.

We are not to be afraid of where we go or what we say when we know we are sent by God. This involves talking to God, knowing Him, learning His language, seeking confirmation of His commands in His Word. When we are in the center of His will, going down a path He has sent us on, there is no reason to be intimidated. However, if we aren't sure He is sending, then we must pause, ask questions, and seek clarification before proceeding. But this, too, involves speaking to God and knowing how to speak to Him. This involves listening to God before we can really listen to others. This involves reading His Word before we can preach His message to others. We must go before His throne and sit at His feet before we can be sent by Him.

Ezekiel 2:1-8, "Stand up and I will speak to you...I am sending you...say to them...do not be afraid (3x's!); you must speak my words to them... listen to what I say to you...open your mouth...go now...speak to them..."

Truths
1. *We must ingest God's Word before we can be sent to speak to others.*

2. *We must listen carefully to all God's commands to obey fully.*

3. *We are not to be afraid when we are sent by God.*

4. *When God says "Go," we go now.*

5. *He won't send us alone, but with help from the Spirit."*

A month later, on July 24th, Kevin and I drove to Atlanta to have the CT scan of my kidneys performed at Emory. This was one medical test that I couldn't have done closer to home, for Emory wanted their staff to perform the scan to their specifications. This test would determine if both kidneys were functioning well enough. Both had to be working and working equally, for one would be given away and needed to be strong enough to sustain my recipient, and the other would be left to sustain me. As always, I wrote in my journal....

"Lord, help the doctors to make the right decision about my kidney donation. Continue to give hope and endurance to my recipient. In a year like 2020, it's easy to be overwhelmed with life, but also sitting on edge waiting for a donor must be excruciating. May they cry out to You in their despair, and may they praise You when they receive the word about a donor stepping forward...

When I was called back for the CT scan and first saw the machine, my anxiety started. I was fine, but my heart was beating a bit faster for the 'unknown'... The machine roared on and spun around me as I was tunneled into it. I closed my eyes and sang worship songs in my head. "It is well with my soul," repeated over and over... for no matter what happens to this body, my soul is well. It is in His hand, always. Pain or not. Comfort or not. Afraid or not.

The roaring stopped, and the machine stopped spinning. I hoped I was done. But then I was told that I was to lay there for 10 minutes, and then they would repeat the scan. So, I played a mental game and recited all the Scripture I knew by heart. All my favorites came to mind: *Jeremiah 29:11,*

Philippians 4, Isaiah 40:31, verses from 1 Peter, John, Genesis, and Isaiah...

I found myself chuckling at one point when I mentally said, "All men are created equal." No, that was the Declaration of Independence, not the Bible! Haha!

But the 10 minutes went by, and the devil stayed away with his branding iron of anxiety. And finally, we repeated the scan.

Normally, when I am stressed, I resort to yoga, breathing, internal praise, or reciting Scripture. But the CT scanning machine would tell me when to breathe in, how long to hold my breath, and when to release. It was a bit different from the rhythm that I would have liked. But nothing can take my Scriptures from me— for they are hidden in my heart—along with some American history, too, apparently.

Finally, the whole thing was done, and I was to return to the lab to have more labs drawn. The lady who drew my blood asked me who I was donating to. I said that I didn't know—that I was just following through with what God instructed me to do, a process I began last December with prayer... The tech's comment was, "With everything bad going on in 2020, and you take it upon yourself to go and do something good."

Isn't that the story of God's redemption for us? That even though we were sinners, Christ died for us. Even though the world was full of bad, Jesus took it upon Himself to sacrifice Himself for the saving of another. And they didn't deserve it. I don't know if my recipient "is worthy" in human eyes of my kidney, and I'm thankful that I do not know them, for my worldview might get in the way.

God sees them as worthy enough. And that is enough for me. It was enough for Christ to come for me, and He knew that I wasn't worthy. But He loved me. And this recipient is loved by God so dearly that God placed this B.I.G. mission on my heart without even knowing them.

Lord, help me to still be obedient, even if it's painful. Please continue to give Kevin peace, for I feel he may be starting to have reservations, but he is leaning on my faith right now. Help him to stand tall in his obedience to Your will as well. I need him to continue to be supportive as a sign to me about an open door to walk through. Last week, with the COVID numbers rising again, I thought he wanted me to cancel this trip, but I had to kiss him and tell him that YOU had to cancel the trip, like you did in April. If you canceled, then ok, but you didn't.

And the kids are involved in an online youth conference this weekend about how everything around us might be canceling, but you don't. You never cancel on us. Ever. Help all our faith grow in this time—mine, my family's, the friends who are watching this from the sidelines, and my recipient. Give him/her hope. Speak life to them. Surround them with believers who are speaking truth and praying for a miracle.

And help my results to show my kidney is worthy of sharing."

At the end of this long journal entry, following my CT scan

at Emory, I was warning myself, *"God-ordained steps of faith are almost always followed by significant opposition and adversity."*

No truer words were spoken. Sure enough, as my "second trimester" closed, my faith was growing exponentially, and my excitement was building, but I was also being divinely prepared for the hardships that the last trimester would entail....

Points to Ponder

1. Read *2 Corinthians 8:9-14*. What are your thoughts on sharing with others? Is God asking you to Be Intentionally Generous in any way or to a certain someone? Carefully pray to God to give you clarity and direction in your acts of generosity.

2. When you find yourself in stressful or anxiety-inducing situations, how do you calm yourself? Have you tried reciting Scripture (and/or historical documents!) to relieve your worries? Has it helped?

3. What are your thoughts on the statement, "God-ordained steps of faith are almost always followed by significant opposition and adversity?"

Devotion: Cast Your Cares On Him
Facebook, Summer 2020

"Lately, I have been digging into 1 Peter in my morning Bible time. Sometimes, you hear or read a verse that you have known for years, but then it takes on a whole new meaning. (That's the beauty of continual study!!)

Well, I was reading *1 Peter 5:7 NIV*, *"Cast all your anxiety on him because he cares for you."* I have boys who like to fish—I mean really like to fish. So, the word 'CAST' is used a lot in my household!

As I was re-reading this verse and thinking about my lil fishermen, I started really understanding it. The definition of 'cast' means 'to throw forcefully in a specified direction.' I don't think anyone will argue with the fact that 2020 (and we are only halfway done!!!) has been full of anxiety and reasons to worry. We started out the year with a near war with Iran, flu season morphed into COVID quarantines, shutdowns, restrictions, unemployment rates, mask debates, school closings and reopenings, riots, and protests, and now we enter hurricane season, and the rest that this beautiful year will throw at us. What are we to do with it ALL????

If we held onto all the anxiety, we would go crazy. We have the potential to become depressed, lash out in anger, mope and cry all day, eat too much, drink too much - or however you personally-handle stress and anxiety...

But what if we CAST it all on God, knowing that He cares about our mental, physical, spiritual, and emotional well-being? What if when life throws things at us, we 'throw it forcefully in a specified direction?' Throw your worries to God; cast them on Him. And like my little fishermen, once you cast your line, you just relax and wait with anticipation for the big catch! And do you know what the BIG catch is every time you cast your anxiety on God?? It is PEACE!

One of my favorite passages in the Bible is **Philippians 4:6-7 NIV.** It has gotten me through a lot of '2020-like' seasons in the past. *"Do not be anxious about anything, but in every situation, by prayer and petition, with thanksgiving, present your requests to God. And the PEACE of God, which transcends all understanding, will guard your hearts and your minds in Christ Jesus."*

Cast your cares, Friends. Though the circumstances may not change, your view of them can - once you cast them out. It doesn't do any good to hold onto them."

18

The Process - "The Third Trimester"

"...For you are a chosen people. You are royal priests, a holy nation, God's very own possession. As a result, you can show others the goodness of God, for he called you out of the darkness into his wonderful light." 1 Peter 2:9 NLT

As my 'third trimester' was beginning, I was feeling the growth of my love for my recipient and the realization that donation was going to happen at some unknown point. I had no idea how short or long this "trimester" was going to be. In addition, I could not have predicted the obstacles that Satan would use to try to stop me.

My canceled mammogram from April finally was rescheduled for the middle of August. On the 19th, I received notice that the results came back abnormal, and another mammogram and ultrasound were necessary. In 2014, when I experienced a breast cancer scare in my early thirties that required a biopsy, God provided everything for me. I was trusting that in 2020, He would continue providing. Honestly, a small part of me was scared, but the rest of me knew this was opposition in response to my obedience, so I prayed and pressed on.

God was with me through this hurdle, and everything

ended up fine. I was not going to take my eyes off the finish line. I journaled....

"Lord, I am all yours. Every part of me. Help me to make healthy decisions to keep me healthy for your purpose. Bless my recipient as they wait and wait and wait some more for this donated kidney. I pray for your perfect timing in this. Remind me to walk by faith, not fear or feelings."

Two days later, on the 21st, I went to the dermatologist. I had a dark freckle on my lip that had been rapidly growing darker all summer, and with a family history of skin cancer, I knew I needed it examined. The doctor did not like how dark it was getting and insisted a biopsy was needed. This was another spiritual attack. Once more, I journaled...

"I started on Monday thinking I might have breast cancer, and now, on Friday, I end the week thinking I could have skin cancer. But... I have a BIG God who has a huge plan for my life. If one little freckle could get in the way of it, then I wouldn't have much faith... I will not fret the small stuff! I will stay focused on my mission. Because yesterday, I also received an especially important email. I am going into the National Kidney Registry!! It is official!.. Once active and matched, it could be just a week til surgery. So, instead of having this mythical surgery looming over my head, I now have excitement that I have run the 2020 race. I have stayed my course - through pandemics, quarantines, CT scans, mammograms, urine samples, blood draws – probably a dozen of them, two different physicals, meetings, emails, pap smear, more blood and urine samples - and now I am on the home stretch of this marathon.

The excitement is building again because I can hear the crowd starting to get louder... I know I am not fighting cancer. I am fighting the devil - one who aims to distract and deter. I am chosen. I am God's special possession."

September 2, 2020, I wrote about how excited I was to give more blood, this time for the CryoKit, the one that would accompany my information into the National Kidney Registry (NKR) and assist doctors in matching me with my recipient. I wrote...

"This is exciting because it feels like we are finally moving forward. When you see God moving, it is exciting, even if there will be pain to endure."

On September 10, I got an email about officially being active. I prayed....

"Continued prayers for God's special someone. May they not lose hope in the waiting."

September 16th...

"Still waiting to hear about a match. Will today be the day? God has a perfect match and perfect timing in mind. Otherwise, He would not have sent me on this journey. Lord, be with the person waiting/struggling/praying for a match. Answer their prayers. Let them see that You see, You care, and You hear their cries."

September 28th...

"I feel lately like I am being spiritually attacked. I have asked Kevin to pray with me more often to protect my heart, mind, and soul. I am not sure if these attacks are Satan getting upset about my witness for Christ or my upcoming surgery (I still have no date). But they must stop in the name of Jesus!

Just moments after writing that last journal entry, in the early morning of September 28th, I took my dogs for their morning walk. While out with them, I received a call from my transplant coordinator stating that I had been matched with a kidney recipient!!! Surgery was set for October 21st!!

This felt like an OB/GYN finally scheduling an induction or C-section. There was a date on the calendar that I could see, count down to, and know that the end was in sight. Yes, discomfort was inevitable, pain and uncertainty as well. But a new life was about to be born, and my own life would forever be changed. I grew incredibly excited as a mother late in her pregnancy awaits delivery.

October 1st...

Today, I fasted breakfast and lunch in prayer. I pray for...
1. My recipient and their health

2. May he/she truly know how much they are loved by Jesus

3. My kids while we are away

4. My health

5. That my recipient will be able to connect with me one day. I want to answer their inevitable question, "Why? Why did you donate?" And I want to be able to tell them...

"Because God loves YOU so much that He nudged me to sacrifice for YOU so that YOU may have life here on Earth. The same very God who sent His one and only son, Jesus, to sacrifice for YOU so that YOU may have eternal life. I wanted to be able to truly show someone what that love really meant. I would not have life if it were not for Jesus, after all. And my body is a temple for the Holy Spirit. I pray my organ can be both a literal and figurative seed planted in the body of another. And I pray that all who work on this side of the country, my friends, my kids' coaches, my doctors and nurses, anyone who hears - and on that side of the country and all connected to my recipient will SEE - some for the very first time - that GOD CARES! He hears. He cares. He acts! Repeatedly in the Bible, the same pattern is there..."

Some people can be TOLD these stories, but others need more physical proof for their faith to develop. I pray that my story - this recipient's story - IS THE PROOF to some-one, anyone, or many, many, someones that God hears. He cares. He acts! After all, *1 Peter 5:7 says, "Cast your cares on God because He cares for YOU."*

October 6th...

Tuesday, I go for the final blood work in the kidney dona-tion process. I also start quarantine - 2 weeks before my COVID test, which is the day before surgery. I will press on to this goal because God has not closed any of these doors yet.

As an altruistic donor, I was able to check one especially important box on a form from my transplant center. It was giving my consent to share my name, phone, and email with my recipient. For communication between donors and recipients to be made, he/she would also need to consent on their end. If both agreed, then after surgeries, personal information about each could be shared. In early October, I checked that box but was also given the opportunity to send along a note to be delivered to my recipient in the event they wanted to read it but did not wish to share their information with me. This was my chance to share my heart before sharing my kidney.

So, on October 16, I composed and sent along a SEVEN-page, typed and single-spaced letter to my recipient. I included many of the journal entries listed earlier in this chapter. I ended the letter with this paragraph....

So, Friend, there you have it. I am sorry for the extreme length of this letter. (My friends and family know I can be quite wordy! LOL) But I truly, truly pray that you are blessed by these words. I have kept track of the 2020 events and my feelings along the way so that you could see GOD in this journey. Here in South Carolina, God has been speaking to me on YOUR behalf. He has swung open doors on YOUR behalf. You are THAT loved! You are THAT worthy. I am not sure if we will be able to have continued correspondence or not, and I am not sure how this health journey will end for either of us, but I will not regret this decision ever. In addition, I would love to hear your side of the journey one day, if at all possible. I will be praying for you continually.

May God bless you always,
Holly Armstrong

Just like a mother about to give birth gently caresses and rubs her bulging belly while speaking soft words of reassurance to her unborn child whom she has grown to love for the last nine months of development inside of her, my heart's desire with this letter was to share Christ's love for my recipient in a way in which he/she could understand. My last 'trimester' was ending, and I could not wait. I knew that Jesus lived in me, and I was about to literally give a piece of myself, Jesus included, to a stranger.

Points to Ponder

1. Have you ever journaled your thoughts, prayers, and concerns during a particular season of life? How has journaling helped you remember God in all the details now that you are in a new season? If you have not and/or do not currently journal, what is stopping you?

2. How would you have felt if you were nearing a major surgery date and about to donate an organ to a stranger? What emotions would you have been feeling?

3. Read *1 Peter 5:7*. Which cares do you need to cast to God today?

Devotion: Searching for the Bigger Picture
Facebook, November 2023

I went out into my gardens today and started to remove fallen leaves and dead plants that did not make it in last week's frost, and then I moved everything to my compost pile. I have always loved getting my hands dirty while talking to God.

While gardening, I was reminded that every freezing frosty night of life does not just kill and destroy - it ushers in a chance for new growth. And what some find as yard 'waste' is the compost needed to help new seeds to grow, to build up the soil for the future seasons.

To be perfectly honest, the last few months have felt like one freezing frosty night after another with various trials my family and I have been through. But God... He keeps reminding me to search for the bigger picture.

Sometimes, it is hard to see the bigger picture when all you see in front of you is the destruction from those trials. But if you look back to remember how God has provided in the past, it is so much easier to have the faith that His plan includes the future as well.

Today, I found healing as I realized how those tough trials have divinely ushered in new growth for my family. The challenging times were not wasted, for they are the experiences building up our faith for future seasons.

I am not sure who needed to hear this today. Perhaps just me. But perhaps someone else can also benefit. Blessings, friends.

"There is a time for everything, and a season for every activity under the heavens:" Ecclesiastes 3:1 NIV

"Dear brothers and sisters, when troubles of any kind come your way, consider it an opportunity for great joy. For you know that when your faith is tested, your endurance has a chance to grow." James 1:2-3 NLT

19

From Cake to Kidney

"So you see, faith by itself isn't enough. Unless it produces good deeds, it is dead and useless. Now someone may argue, "Some people have faith; others have good deeds." But I say, "How can you show me your faith if you don't have good deeds? I will show you my faith by my good deeds." James 2:17-18 NLT

As an educator, I see the benefit of the testing process. Without assessing a student's knowledge of a subject matter, it is hard for a teacher to evaluate what the student does or does not understand. However, when I was a student in high school and college, tests used to create anxiety in me. I felt so much pressure to answer every question correctly. Inevitably, though, 100% on every single test in every single subject was impossible. I felt like a failure every time a bright red "X" appeared next to a test question I did not understand. From a student's perspective, tests can be horrid, but from a teacher's perspective, they are helpful. It took me many, many years to learn from my mistakes, both on tests and in real life, and to see them as catalysts for better achievements next time. I have a memory of one mistake that forever changed me, and thankfully, from which I learned a great deal.

Early on in my walk with Christ, when I was a newlywed of college, I remember running into Costco one day for a gallon of milk. We used to live in Maryland, about a mile from Costco, so I often found myself dropping in after work for just 1 or 2 items. This particular trip was a rushed one. I had been in a hurry for some reason, so I grabbed the milk and quickly hopped in line and found myself behind a massively pregnant lady who was buying a large sheet cake.

The cashier asked the lady for her payment, and she began digging around in her purse for what seemed like an eternity. Finally, she found her wallet and handed the cashier a credit card. Upon swiping the card, the cashier said that the card had been denied. The pregnant lady said she would have to leave to withdraw cash and then return for the cake.

In my selfishness, I became frustrated at how long this transaction was taking. But I heard a still, small voice in my head whispering, *"Buy the cake for her."*

At this stage of my faith, my heart was not in tune with the voice of God, and honestly, I was still more focused on myself rather than others. I debated the thought in my head for a few seconds. I was thinking that Costco cakes are quite cheap, that I could probably make this lady's day a heck of a lot easier by simply purchasing the cake for her, and so forth. But I had taken too long to decide; the lady had already left, and I missed my opportunity.

I stepped forward, bought my milk, and left, but not without glancing at the cake that still sat there unpurchased. It was decorated for a little child, a toddler's birthday. That lady was probably so stressed that day, planning a party at the end of her third trimester, and I could have helped but chose not to.

While walking to my car with the milk that I no longer seemed to want, I felt like a failure. God had asked me to do something so simple, but I had not been willing. Sure, God is all-powerful, and if I chose to disobey Him, He could have easily provided for that lady by using someone more obedient. I believe this test was given so I could realize how much I still needed to learn about obedience. I needed to learn to trust God more, listen to His voice more closely, remove distractions and the "what if" scenarios, and to simply obey when asked.

This memory has lived with me since. I still think of that "Costco test" often when God asks me to give anything away or to do something for someone. And I was thinking of that test as I was preparing to go to surgery in October 2020.

By that new stage in my faith, 17 years after my "Costco test," I knew God loved me. I no longer thought that I had to earn my salvation. I knew that I would make mistakes, and God would graciously forgive me again and again and again.

I also knew what obedience meant. I had spent the last 15 years of parenthood teaching this very concept. I always taught Ellie, Ben, and Sammy that obedience needed to be three things:

1. Immediate

2. Complete

3. Cheerful

I would use the example that if I asked them to put their laundry away, they were to complete that task today, not tomorrow or next week. *Psalm 119:60 NLT* says, *"I will hurry, without delay, to obey your commands."* Doing something delayed is not fully obeying.

They were also to put all their laundry away. If they only put their shirts away but left their pants and socks, that would not be complete obedience. The Israelites suffered for generations because they did not fully obey God's initial commands when they first entered the Promised Land.

And my children were instructed to obey cheerfully. Stomping their feet up the stairs to their room and slamming their doors to put the laundry away would not be cheerful obedience.

The Bible says in **2 Corinthians 9:7 NIV** that *"…God loves a cheerful giver"*

My entire 2020 had been spent trying to fully obey God in this new mission—one where He asked me to donate my kidney to a complete stranger. I felt humbled that He would use me in this way, and I wanted to quickly, completely, and cheerfully obey Him, not to earn His love but as an expression of my love for Him. I will say it was a much bigger test than buying a cake for someone at Costco.

On October 18th, Kevin and I said goodbye to the children. We had arranged for numerous close friends and neighbors to help chauffeur the kids to their practices, drop off meals, and be around in case of an emergency. This was the first time we were leaving them for five days all by themselves. Ellie was about to turn 15, Ben was almost 13, and Sammy was 11.

I vividly remember standing in the front yard, giving them all hugs as we said our goodbyes. I asked to take a few family selfies. Inwardly, I knew that there was a chance that this would be the last time I would see them. I had never had any surgeries before besides having my wisdom teeth extracted. And yes, kidney donations have become increasingly advanced, but surgery is still surgery. There are always risks that serious complications could occur, no matter how small the chance is. Having grown up without a father, I prayed that my children would not lose their mother.

As soon as we drove away, all my inner fears and last anxieties gave way to sobs, wet, messy, heart-wrenching sobs. At one point, Kevin asked me if he should turn around. I continued to cry but motioned with my hands to simply keep moving forward. I later journaled about those first moments of that drive…

"I was strong for the kids, but I cried the first 20 minutes of the trip. I could not stop thinking that they might never see me again. I know the chances are slim, but there is risk.

And it finally hit me what I was possibly putting them through. But I have friends praying for me, and I felt those prayers, and God's peace flooded my soul."

The next morning, I had to pass a COVID test and have final labs drawn. The tech who administered the test asked me if I was "giving" or "getting" a kidney. I journaled about this conversation...

"As always, when asked if I was giving a kidney, the next question is always "to whom?" And as always, when I respond that I do not know, I get a shocked, wide-eyed stare as people attempt to process that information. The tech said, "I don't understand." I then sat with her for 20 minutes, telling her my story and my journey. She said she thought that she was meant to hear from me today. She asked me, "How do I get that much faith?" I replied by telling her it was by spending more time talking and listening to Jesus. I said that my kids would never know that I wanted them to do the dishes if they weren't close enough to hear me ask that of them or if they didn't spend the time listening to what I had to say. It is the same thing listening to what God is saying in your life..."

Being all ready for surgery to take place on Wednesday, October 21st, I wrote in my journal one last time on the night of the 20th. As you can see, I was completely and utterly excited. I had no more fear, anxiety, or hesitation. I was about to undergo my first-ever surgery and experience the most intense physical pain that I had ever endured, but I felt perfectly centered in God's will for my life, and that put me on cloud nine...

"I feel like Johnny Appleseed just planting seeds as I travel down this journey God has placed me on. It is sooooo much bigger than just my recipient. It is all the people I encounter who SEE Jesus at work in me. It is all the people on the sidelines and spectators watching this "game God has put me in." Some are cheering for God, the winning team. Others might cheer for the enemy. But God is winning and will continue to win. I had prayed to be taken off the bench and put in the game. God had faith in me, and I have faith in Him. It is too grand to put into words. I wish more people would stop loving the status quo life and seek the enjoyment of "Being in the Game." There is not much better than to play. Fans are the ones who cannot play, are not good enough, are not asked to be on a team, or are retired from playing. But players - they are the ones scoring the points! With God giving me the plays, there is no way I will lose. What an honor and privilege to be put in this game."

Though this entire book is about my personal experience of learning to trust and obey, it is imperative that one realize my supporting character, the love of my life, and his journey as well. Kevin's faith journey parallels mine in so many ways. But the testing of his faith was not walking into the operating room, it was dropping me off at Emory at 4:00 am on October 21st and driving away. Due to COVID restrictions, Emory forbade all visitors. He was not allowed to hold my hand as I waited. He did not have the hope of laying eyes on me as I awoke from surgery. No, he simply had to drop me off and drive back to a hotel room and attempt to work remotely for the next three days until a nurse called him saying I was ready for discharge. His faith on the morning of my surgery is one of the greatest examples of a quiet, strong faith that I have ever witnessed.

Surgery only lasted a few short hours. I remember waking up out of anesthesia, throwing a wild tantrum through shrieks and tears about how much pain I was in. I vaguely remember them calling Kevin and getting permission for a nerve block to be administered. I later remember being wheeled to my room, the one where my extroverted self was dreading staying in for three days all by myself. *"Stupid COVID restrictions,"* I thought; I wanted my husband by my side!

For the last few months, I had been praying big prayers, HUGE prayers. Besides the prayers for my children whom we left home for the week, prayers for my recipient's health, and prayers for my own safety, I prayed that somehow, just somehow, God would show me favor and allow Kevin to visit me in the hospital. I had asked numerous times to everyone I encountered at all my pre-op appointments, and they were all incredibly sorry, but he was simply not allowed in.

However, I remembered reading that in rare circumstances, a visitor could be admitted for the unruliest of patients, so I joked with my recovery nurse, *"What kind of fit would I have to throw to get my husband allowed access to visit me?"*

The nurse chuckled but apologized and reiterated that no visitors were allowed.

Ephesians 3:20 NIV describes God as *"...**Him who is able to do immeasurably more than all we ask or imagine...**"* And my God did immeasurably more! A nursing assistant "happened" to walk into the room at that exact time and overheard my question and the nurse's answer. She spoke up and said that she had just finished reading an email that said Emory changed their policy, and TODAY was the very first day they were allowing visitors again. Cases were rising at this time, so it did not make sense! Even though I had prayed for it, I did not really think that Kevin would be able to visit, let alone move in and be with me for the next three days. But that is what he did. God had proven once more that He cares about the littlest details in one's life.

It was so lovely to have Kevin by my side. He instantly

made me more comfortable rather than waiting for a nurse to come anytime I needed assistance. His 6'3" frame squeezed onto a 5-foot hospital couch for the next two nights without any words of complaint. He, too, was simply thankful to be by my side. His love for me, through his gentle acts of service during that recovery and the weeks that followed, truly served me like the hands and feet of Jesus.

The first evening in recovery, my surgeon came to check on me. He shared with us a picture of my kidney that he took after removing it. He said the surgery was slightly difficult due to my petite frame, but all went well. I, however, simply wanted to know more about my recipient and if he had any information he could share. He informed us that the kidney had already safely flown from Atlanta to Los Angeles and was successfully transplanted into my recipient's body. I also learned that my kidney had gone to another mother and that she was doing well.

Oh, that sweet, joyful news was like hearing, "It's a girl! And she has ten fingers and ten toes!" Finally, I knew the gender of my recipient, and I knew that she was healthy. Both surgeries were successful. That satisfied my soul so well! It was another example of God doing immeasurably more.

God had initially laid donation on my heart because I felt empathy for a mother. I had thought it was a mother who had a sick child, and my kidney would save the child. But no, the feelings I had when I sobbed my way to Atlanta just days before, wondering if my children were going to lose their mother, were the feelings God really wanted me to experience. He knew there was a mother 3,000 miles away who was in desperate need to be there for her child or children. He was using my kidney to bless her with more time with her family.

Recovery in the hospital was exhausting, and I could not wait to be discharged just to be able to sleep through the night in my own bed. The four-hour drive home was tense, feeling every bump in my freshly dissected abdomen, but I was thrilled to finally go home and hug my own children again.

When I started the donation journey, I was just taking one step forward in the direction God pointed. I honestly did not know if it would end in surgery. But throughout the entire process, I learned the greatest lesson He had been trying to teach me all along. Yes, my recipient in California needed a kidney, but He could have asked a multitude of more faithful and qualified saints to donate. But He had asked me. Why? What this donor needed most was to learn to trust Him in everything. For me, it was not the destination but the reliance on my Savior throughout the entire journey that was the test that I had finally learned to pass.

By the way, two years after my surgery, I found myself in my Bible study sharing my Costco story. I shared how I would love to go back in time and help that pregnant lady in Costco. A few days after sharing my heart, I found myself at Walmart. I had run in to purchase an item and found myself behind - get this - a very pregnant lady buying groceries. I was smiling and playing peekaboo with the lady's toddler (fellow extroverts will understand!) while the mother placed her groceries on the conveyor belt. I then heard the cashier give the final total to the mother, who looked surprised at the amount, saying she did not expect it to cost that much. She started to apologize to the cashier that she would need to put back a few items, for she did not have that much in her account. I overheard God giving me a sweet, redemptive opportunity. Within the blink of an eye, I found myself inserting my debit card and telling the cashier that I would take care of the bill. The pregnant mother had tears in her eyes as she thanked me. Looking at her with my own watery eyes, I simply told her that God loved her and that He loved me, too, by giving me the pleasure of helping her that day.

Friends, are you trusting God enough to obey Him in the little and the massive things He asks of you? My prayer is that you might learn from the past times when you may have failed to obey and earnestly seek to obey Him the next time He asks you to do good and share with those in need.

Points to Ponder

1. How has God provided for you in your life in immeasurable ways?

2. What prayer do you have today where you can ask God to do the immeasurable?

3. Have you ever considered that you, too, can be a Johnny Appleseed and plant seeds of faith wherever you go? Who could benefit from hearing your personal testimony?

4. Read **Hebrews 13:16**. How could you share with someone today?

Devotion: We Love Because He First Loved Us
Facebook, November 18, 2020

Love. Oftentimes, people think they need to earn love. They think they must DO something to deserve the attention and love of others. No, true love comes when it is needed... Stays with you during your hardest times... Holds you close... Fights for you... Speaks up for you... Is simply there for you... Regardless. It is just up to us to believe that the love is real and choose to accept it.

The same is true with God. God loves us because He created us. We did not have to DO anything to deserve his attention or affection. He came when we needed Him most - and provided a plan to be with us.... save us.... fight for us.... speak up for us.... to hold us closely. It is just up to us to believe that His love is real and choose to receive it.

The last few weeks have been super hard, I won't lie. I often post about family birthdays or kids' milestones because I hate adding more sadness to this world, but instead, I try to add joy and laughter to the lives of others through 'happy posts' in their feeds.

But planning for, traveling for, having, and recovering from major surgery has not been easy. (Totally worth it, and I would do it again, but it still wasn't easy!)

It was not simply hard on me, but also on my family, and my close friends, who have bent over backwards to help. (I sooo appreciate you!!)

My sweet husband, however, gets the GOLD for displaying true love during this time. He has not once complained. He has not once gotten frustrated. He has not once turned his back on me.

No, he was able to show me true love because his heart is connected to the Source of Love.

"We love because God loved us first." 1 John 4:19 CEV

Want to love your family better? Want to love your spouse better? Want to love others better? Draw close to the one who IS love and learn more about true love. Then, it will just naturally flow out of you, even during the most difficult of times. People around you will notice, and it will draw them also to the source of Love. Truth.

20

My Recipient

"The Lord bless you and keep you; the Lord make his face shine on you and be gracious to you; the Lord turn his face toward you and give you peace." Numbers 6:24-26 NIV

Kelley Rivera, whom God loved enough to intervene in my life on her behalf, was the sweet soul who received my kidney on the afternoon of October 21, 2020. I initially knew her as merely the unnamed stranger God wanted to bless through my sacrificial obedience.

Within a few hours of my surgery, I knew her as a mother from California who now used my kidney to filter blood through her physical body. But in God's immeasurable answer to my months of heartfelt prayers, within a month of surgery, I knew her as Kelley, a spunky Certified Public Accountant who was about 15 years older than me, a mother of one adult daughter, Morgan, and loving wife to Peter.

Within milliseconds of first speaking with Kelley, I knew I had given up a kidney to honor God, but He, in return, had gifted me with a new dear, dear friend whom I grew to know and love deeply.

When life comes from one body and enables another body

to live, there is a special bond that is immediately formed. Anyone who has ever become a parent would understand the instantaneous love for a stranger upon hearing their voice for the first time and gazing upon their face. On Zoom with Kelley that first time, we giggled so much. We never, ever felt like we were strangers. Instead, we felt like friends that needed to catch up on each other's lives. Over time, we would spend hours upon hours on FaceTime, Zoom, texting, emailing, calling, and Facebook messaging. We learned so much about each other.

When Kelley was just six years old, she was diagnosed with Type 1 Diabetes. Her mother first realized something was wrong during bath time one evening. She noticed how Kelley's ribs stuck out, for she had been losing weight rapidly and seemed unable to absorb the nutrients from the food she consumed. This was the first noticeable sign of juvenile diabetes. In addition, Kelley urinated frequently. Both early warning symptoms led Kelley's mother to take Kelley to her pediatrician. Upon checking Kelley's blood sugar levels that very first time, the pediatrician ordered Kelley to head straight to the hospital, for her blood sugar levels were over 700! Kelley's father stayed with her at the hospital that night. It took the medical staff nine painful attempts to start an IV on her, which would be the very beginning of a painful and scary lifetime of dealing with this horrible disease.

Kelley was the oldest of three siblings. Her younger brother and sister would also inadvertently be affected by Kelley's condition. Sugary drinks and treats in their household needed to be strictly monitored. Kelley's parents would spend countless hours devoted to Kelley and her disease, learning how to check her blood sugar levels, administering insulin shots, and driving Kelley to and from endless doctors' appointments and hospital stays throughout her childhood.

During the 1970's, there was no help or organization that was designed to help parents of diabetic children. Kelley's mother recalls struggling with learning everything. She remembered one holiday season that Kelley was having a blood sugar episode and the doctor on call suggested an incorrect dosage for Kelley to receive. He had miscalculated it in the wrong direction, suggesting Kelley get twice as much instead of half. Thankfully, Kelley's parents' gut instinct told them to disregard his advice. They calculated their own dosage and saved Kelley's life, for had they administered the erroneously prescribed one, they would have inadvertently killed their beloved firstborn.

Over the course of Kelley's childhood, she struggled to regulate her blood sugar with this disease. She went into comas because the technology of having pumps did not exist at the time. Her parents gave her two shots daily to help the insulin run smoothly through her body, but long-term damage to Kelley's organs could not be avoided.

As an adult, Kelley not only struggled with regulating her blood sugar but also with numerous eye infections and heart attacks due to her disease. By the time she was older, Kelley would be given a pump that would replicate her malfunctioning pancreas, creating a constant flow of insulin in her body, but years of damage had already occurred. Over time, diabetes can leave one with vision problems, and Kelley was not exempt from this side effect. She suffered from vision changes, eye pressure, and eye infections. She would have hours-long eye doctor appointments, and often the eye issues would interfere with her ability to work, especially during tax season as a CPA. In addition, Kelley suffered multiple heart attacks, beginning at the age of 40. Doctors told her parents and husband that Kelley would not live to reach her 50th birthday, for the diabetes was wreaking havoc on too many of Kelley's organs.

However, Kelley would receive my kidney at the age of 56, beating the odds that were medically stacked against her. God is more powerful than any diagnosis, and He had plans for Kelley and me to intersect paths. In August of 2019, due to the damage done to her kidneys, it was determined that Kelley would need to travel down one of two paths - lifelong dialysis or seek a kidney transplant.

Kelley and Peter began investigating what dialysis would look like. Kidneys filter a person's blood, and when they stop functioning, dialysis can help perform that necessary function, but it requires being connected to a machine for a minimum of four hours three times a day. Kelley and Peter decided this would not work for them! They refused to even consider dialysis and began investigating transplant options. The waitlist is long for those in need of a transplant, lasting around five years. Seeking a donor can be time-consuming and heart-wrenching while one's organs slowly fail the body.

However, the wait can be shortened if a friend or family member volunteers to be evaluated. Potential donors must undergo rigorous testing to see if their kidneys would be compatible with Kelley and whether their bodies can withstand the surgery and the lasting effects of living with one kidney. Many potential donors are eliminated daily due to high blood pressure, obesity, kidney cysts, and other medical conditions.

For Kelley, multiple blood relatives agreed to get evaluated to see if they were a match for her. Over the next several months, they each went through various stages of the screening process. Ultimately, it seemed as if her brother would be the best match. But long story short, her brother was willing to donate, but the doctors would not medically allow him to do so. As Kelley said, "It ended up that he had one great kidney, and one kidney wasn't as good, so they didn't want to put that kidney in me."

Peter, though not a direct match for Kelley, was cleared to donate due to his two highly functioning kidneys. This led Peter and Kelley down a different path than they initially sought. Peter was willing to do anything to avoid dialysis for his wife. So, he stepped up to donate his kidney to a stranger on the waiting list. In exchange, UCLA Health, where Kelley was registered on the national transplant list, would bump Kelley up to the top of the waiting list. This is an exchange program that many utilize when capable but incompatible family members are willing to donate to loved ones. Peter was hoping to avoid a long, drawn-out wait for his wife, who would need dialysis to stay alive while she waited.

With thirty-two years of marriage to Kelley and a heart full of love, Peter donated his kidney to a stranger on September 23, 2020, moving Kelley to the top of the transplant list.

Just two days later, as Peter was being discharged from the hospital from his surgery, Kelley's transplant coordinator called her, saying that she had found a match for Kelley...me. Kelley said...

> "She thought it was too good to be true, so she said, "Well, let me take the weekend and evaluate it and look at it Monday with fresh eyes." Then on Monday, the transplant coordinator called and said, "Kelley, this is a perfect match. The donor is AB positive like you; the donor is alive, and the donor is young. It is a Disneyland Match.""

God is all over Kelley's story, even though she did not notice it at first. She wrote to me in November 2021 when I asked a few questions about her past kidney issues. She said....

> "When I had my Morgan in 1992, they told me I had 5-7 years left on my kidney. But I didn't listen to them. I had the kidney transplant 28 years later. I have always watched my kidneys through blood work every three months, but the problem escalated in 2019 where I had to consider options... The irony with my kidney issues is that most people would have been hospitalized with the numbers I was running. I

felt fine and worked full-time. I had no symptoms except for my blood work numbers. But your kidney was a PERFECT match!"

God, in His infinite wisdom, had perfectly directed and timed my steps so that Kelley and I would connect, and my kidney donated to her specifically. It is profoundly humbling to have been used by God in this manner, and I am so thankful for His bigger picture. Had her brother or Peter been direct matches for Kelley, she would have received a kidney but may not have felt God's love behind the gift that God directed me to give. And the stranger who received Peter's kidney would not have received his gift of sacrifice either. Jesus shows us repeatedly in the Gospels of the New Testament that He cares not just about physical healing but spiritual healing as well. For example, in Matthew 9, Jesus not only healed the paralyzed man but also forgave him of his sins. In John 11, Jesus rose Lazarus from the dead to reveal God's glory to the crowd that had gathered, for He cared more about the eternal than the temporary. And of course, in Jesus' own crucifixion and resurrection, He demonstrated His love for all to receive spiritual healing.

Medically, Kelley and I were quite different, for I had grown up with the privilege of health, and my kidney donation was my first surgery, but spiritually, we were vastly different as well. Kelley's parents were of Jewish background but were not ones to practice Judaism or pass the traditions down to their children. Kelley and her family would celebrate Passover every year with a practicing aunt, but that time together was centered around the importance of family, not necessarily faith. Kelley recalled never having had any spiritual training growing up, for her father had even become an atheist. When Kelley married Peter, who came from a Catholic background, they would have Morgan baptized in the Catholic church, but only after Kelley's father passed away. Together, they raised her without any specific spiritual training, for both Kelley and Peter were fairly agnostic.

Kelley and I would speak of God together frequently. She had an earnest desire to understand my WHY behind donation, and with faith being the main theme to that answer, we often talked about God. Despite not initially believing in God herself, she questioned me constantly about my beliefs. Her inquiries never felt aggressive or condescending. Instead, I felt that she sincerely wanted to understand something that was so completely foreign to anything she had ever experienced. And with my heart's desire to know my recipient and to share my faith with them, this became a natural conversation topic of ours.

Kelley often would tell me how thankful she was to me for having given her my kidney. Humbly, I had to constantly redirect her gratitude to the One who directed me to donate. I would remind her that I honestly would never have donated had God not told me to do so. I was even more bluntly honest with her, saying that if I were given a list of those waiting on the transplant list, I probably would not have chosen to donate to her directly, for I thought God wanted me to donate to a child, not someone in their 50's. But God.... But God perfectly matched the two of us together!

With Kelley and with anyone else who has asked me, I often use the example of a grandmother mailing her grandchild a birthday card and money. When the gift is received in the mail, the grandchild does not hug the mail carrier, repeatedly telling him thank you for the birthday present. No, they pick up the telephone and call the grandmother who sent the gift to thank her directly. I constantly reminded Kelley of this, asking her to please stop thanking me, but instead thank God who sent me. And within two months of conversing, she wrote to me once while sick, *"Can you pray for me, please? See - you did change me!"*

For the first time, Kelley acknowledged the existence of

God and the power of prayer. She knew that I would pray to God on her behalf. Within a year, Kelley began praying herself, bringing me immeasurable joy. She wrote to me saying, *"I thanked God today for the kidney you gave me."*

Kelley once told me that she enjoyed reading the Children's Bibles found in the waiting rooms of many of her doctor's offices growing up. She had been a gifted, intelligent child. God used her inclination to read, her boredom while waiting, the need for repetitive appointments, and perfectly placed Bibles to slowly plant seeds in her heart for His Word.

For Kelley's first birthday after donation, I ordered her a large print version of the Message Bible. In God's divine plan, I accidentally had it shipped to my own address instead of hers. Initially, I felt silly for the mistake, but I prayed about it. God told me to read through it first and give it my personal touch before sending it to her. So secretly, from July to December that year, I read through her new Bible, highlighting favorite passages throughout the whole thing. I wrote her little notes in there as well. And for Christmas 2021, I sent her that Bible. She wrote to me on Christmas Eve...

"The large print bible will be so much easier on my tired eyes - what a great idea! I will smile and think of you when I use it. Thank you so much!"

On my birthday, two years after our surgeries, Kelley publicly posted on my Facebook page for all to see, *"Happy birthday to a beautiful gift from **Jesus** who gave me life, hope, and the ability to see more sunsets..."*

It took her time to grasp and many, many hours of explaining over the phone, but Kelley admitted to me on multiple occasions, *"You have changed how I view God,"* and *"I love viewing God from your perspective."*

This. This is why I donated! God had done immeasurably more than I could have ever asked in not only giving me a dear,

dear friend in Kelley, but also allowing me to guide her to the Father who loved her so much more than she ever realized. To hear her talking about God, praying to Him, thanking Him, and even publicly speaking the name of Jesus brought me incredible joy! Yes, God had much grander plans for Kelley and my kidney. It was not so much about her physical health, but I genuinely believe it was a plan for her spiritual healing as well.

Besides sharing my faith with Kelley, we enjoyed hearing about each other's lives. We would constantly message one another about what was happening with our families. On November 28, 2021, she messaged me...

"Do you remember one of the reasons I was so thankful that you donated your incredible kidney to me? I would be able to walk Morgan down the aisle at her wedding. She told us on Thanksgiving that they are ring shopping! It's a huge secret and you are the only person that I've told. Just another reason to be thankful for you and your beautiful spirit... And I love that you're the first person I wanted to share this with!"

With being a sports mama, I often would use the time spent waiting for my boys to finish their lacrosse practices to give Kelley a call. I remember sitting at the field one day, learning all about the wedding planning. Kelley's joy with helping plan the wedding was contagious. She would go on and on describing the flowers, the dress, the venue, and every other detail that went into preparing her only child's special day. She admittedly struggled with the idea of inviting me out to the wedding, though. She said she did not want our first in-person meeting to be at a time when she would have been so distracted with being the mother of the bride. I completely understood. I wanted Kelley to focus on nothing else besides her beautiful daughter on her special day. Kelley even sent me a video sneak peek of Morgan in her gown the day they decided on which to purchase. She loved having me to share those things with since I could keep a secret and did not know the rest of the family yet. Plus, we both knew that it was the gift of my kidney that was enabling Kelley to be part of this momentous occasion. She loved sharing these intricate details with me.

I still remember sitting at my son's lacrosse practice in May 2023, a few days after the wedding, when my phone rang, and Kelley and I chatted for well over an hour about how wonderful of a night it was. With our surgeries occurring during COVID, and with Kelley's intense desire to protect her gifted kidney and ultimately her health (especially while on the necessary post-transplant immunosuppressant drugs), she was intensely strict with whom she exposed herself. Admittedly, she became reclusive, only eating in outdoor venues, only seeing family who could prove they had not been exposed to illnesses, and even storing Amazon packages outside for days before opening them, just in case. But Morgan's wedding was a different story. She spent the night dancing and seeing long-lost friends and relatives. She was on cloud nine and could not wait to share every single detail with me. Her heart was bursting with joy, and it radiated through my cell phone. I was so happy for her, Peter, and the rest of their family.

Next, Kelley and I discussed possibilities about finally meeting each other in person. We talked through numerous scenarios and plans. We both could not wait to hug each other, but COVID and her health concerns, the 3,000 miles that separated us, her daughter's wedding plans, my family's mission trips and vacations, my daughter's high school graduation, and so much more seemed to keep pushing the date further back.

In July 2023, I would finally get to travel to California to meet Kelley and her family, but unfortunately, not under the circumstances we envisioned.

Points to Ponder

1. Have you ever met someone with whom you had an instantaneous bond? What was that like, and what did you bond over?

2. How do you see God's provision for Kelley over her lifetime struggles with diabetes?

3. If you were to meet someone new, would they say, "I love seeing God through your eyes?" If so, what would you share with them? If not, what is holding you back from sharing God with others?

Devotion: Uniquely Designed

Written for Community Bible Study Leaders, November 19, 2021

Have any of you ever heard of the amygdala? I am guessing since most of you aren't brain surgeons, you might not know too much about it. Do not worry; I didn't know much about it initially either. I want to share with you what I have learned about the amygdala while reminding you of the awesome creativity God uses when designing each person's unique story.

So, here is your quick science lesson: The amygdala is one of two almond-shaped clusters of nuclei that are located deep within the temporal lobes of the brain's cerebrum. All you really need to know is that the amygdala is responsible for a person's ability to process emotional responses, such as empathy.

In the last decade or so, a few scientists started studying the amygdala in greater detail. They wanted to compare people who had a 'missing sense of empathy' and those who had a 'heightened sense of empathy.' So, they studied psychopaths and altruistic donors (ones who have donated organs to complete strangers.) The psychopaths are those who seem to be missing a sense of empathy, perhaps from trauma to the brain or other causes such as tumors or cysts prohibiting the development of the amygdala, while altruistic donors are on the opposite end, with massively elevated senses of empathy. With being such a donor, I was intrigued when I started reading about this research.

Scientists have discovered that altruistic donors seem to have enlarged amygdalas. The Los Angeles Times newspaper even published an article with the headline, "Brains of Kidney Donors Seem Built for Generosity." The causes for the enlarged amygdala are still up for debate. Were these individuals born that way, or was there a reason the amygdala grew to an enlarged size?

Regardless, this is where I really started digging into the research to learn more. Science estimates that only 1% of the population has this unique difference in their brain, and this might explain why not everyone is knocking on surgeons' doors begging to have an organ removed.

With our mini science completed, lets dig into my personal history...Throughout my whole life, as long as I can remember, I have always felt different. I would cry at commercials. I would have the inability to read stories aloud to my children without becoming choked up. I have even sobbed my way through history lessons while homeschooling because it was so hard for me to learn about the trials of others without putting myself in their shoes and feeling their emotions. I simply was designed to feel deeply.

Another fact about me was that I was born with AB+ blood. It is the second rarest blood type in the United States, with less than 4% of the population having it.

And one last fact that helps tie everything together... prior to 2020, my husband, Kevin, traveled often for work. He would take, on average, at least two or three trips a month. But between February 2020 and November 20202, he took zero trips. None. In fact, COVID restrictions forbade him from even going into his office, and he worked from home that entire time.

Now, a theology lesson. I passionately believe that as Christians, we need to investigate the details of our lives a bit more than we probably do on a daily basis. I know that whenever I pause to consider the vast creativity God uses in putting things together, my mind is blown away. *Psalm 119:15 NIV* says, *"I meditate on your precepts and consider your ways."*

Had I not "paid close attention to all His ways," I would not be able to share what I discovered when I put science, history, and theology all together. God knit me together in my mother's womb or allowed at an early age the increased growth of my amygdala. He gave my brain a unique design, one for heightened empathy, and He created me with an uncommon blood type designed to perfectly match me with a complete stranger in need 3,000 miles away 40 years later. That alone blows my mind. Then, God allowed my husband's company to freeze all travel for 21 months - the exact months I would need extra help in chauffeuring kids to their activities and homeschooling them while I went to doctor after doctor after doctor's appointments to clear me for my donation surgery. And then, I not only had him in town but in the house to help when I needed to recover from three different surgeries.

So, just like God parted the Red Sea or stopped the flow of the Jordan for the Israelites to cross and then restarted it when they were safely to the other side, God stopped Kev's busy traveling for the season I needed him most, and then restarted once I had 'crossed my Jordan.'

So many minute details, so many intricate workings of God. I would need to draft a book to list them all (and who knows, maybe I will one day).

I just want to encourage you to pause and consider God's ways and to offer thanksgiving to Him. You may not have AB+ blood and an enlarged amygdala, and you also might not be asked by God to donate a kidney. I am, however, positive that God has uniquely designed each of you for the purpose He has in mind FOR YOU.

Every experience you have been through and every unique DNA trait that you possess has been perfectly designed to create the masterpiece that you are. And all we need to do is simply pause and thank Him for paying such close attention to the details in our individual lives, even the things we might find insignificant. Nothing is insignificant to God. He has been, and will always be, at work in your life. How amazingly cool is that?!?!

21

The Unexpected Meeting

"Blessed are those who mourn, for they will be comforted."
Matthew 5:4 NIV

Sometimes, humans make plans, but the Lord creates vastly different paths from those plans. It is during those times that our faith is evaluated the deepest. One must ask themself if they undoubtedly trust God. If they don't, they can get lost trying to follow their own way. This was something I had unfortunately tried in my later teen and early college years, but then I found myself hopeless and alone. And ever since, I have learned that my only choice is to follow closely to God, down any path, and experience the protection of his presence. Sometimes, those paths, however, can be very, very dark valleys.

The summer of 2023 was full of change and all sorts of emotions. My firstborn had graduated high school. We did it; the great 'homeschool experiment' had been successful! Ellie graduated high school a year early, earned a full tuition scholarship to attend a small Christian private school only two hours away from home, and was following Jesus closely. It brought me so much joy and relief to know that I had not messed up that poor firstborn guinea pig with the crazy idea of homeschooling her all the way through. Her success gave me the needed confidence and hope to continue with her brothers, who were only a few short years behind her in graduating themselves.

A handful of experienced homeschooling friends and I spent the summer following God's call to start a brand-new cooperative that would help other homeschooling parents in our area educate their children. Although this was time-consuming and stressful, we each felt confident that it was what God was asking of us.

Additionally, there was a major scandal at the church we had been attending. It involved the arrest of a pastor, knowledge of harm done to close friends, and the possibility that my children had potentially been preyed upon. This caused us incredible stress and the need to cling to Jesus even tighter as we wrestled with forgiveness and more. All this was concurrently happening when I received an unexpected call in July.

Kelley's birthday is July 29th, which is easy for me to remember since it is also my mother's birthday. Our family had plans to vacation in the West Virginian mountains without cell service or internet. We desperately needed to "unplug" and spend quality time together, so I preemptively sent Kelley her birthday presents early, and we agreed to chat on the phone after I returned.

On Sunday, July 23rd as we packed to leave for the mountains, I was not expecting to hear from Kelley. However, I absolutely loved seeing her name pop up on my cell phone. So, when I answered, I bubbly exclaimed, *"Well, hi, my kidney buddy!!! How are you??"*

I heard Peter's voice on the other end of the line, and I intuitively knew something was seriously wrong. I figured Kelley had fallen ill and was perhaps in the hospital. It was worse, and I was not prepared to hear the worst. Peter, as stoic as he always is, simply told me what had just occurred. Kelley had not been feeling well for the last few days, but she refused to go to the emergency room, for she hated being there. But finally, that morning, she had agreed to have Peter take her, but she wanted to take a shower first. Kelley then collapsed in her bathroom from a heart attack. Peter attempted CPR and called the medics, but Kelley was gone. Her kidney had done its job, but her heart had suffered too much stress from all those years of diabetes wreaking havoc on her organs.

I was in complete shock at hearing that account. I did not know what else to do or to say, but I remember asking Peter if I could pray with him. He agreed. I do not remember the words I prayed, but I remember wanting to use this precious moment with Peter to help him draw near to God, the only one who could help in this terrible time of shock and grief. I knew that Kelley had begun seeking God and praying, but I didn't know anything of Peter's spiritual health. I prayed that God would give him peace that passes all understanding.

In my grief, I prayed repeatedly for Kelley's relatives and anyone else who was struggling with her loss. My peace came when God reminded me that His ways are always higher. He spoke to my heart and said, *"Go to them. Tell them of my love for them, the way you have shared it with Kelley."*

"God, I'm not sure."

"Trust me."

"God, the funeral is the same day my boys are both scheduled to have their wisdom teeth out. The last-minute flights are so expensive. The family does not even know me. Will they even want me there? I do not want to cause them any stress. I simply don't know."

"Trust me. I will always provide. Be strong and courageous. You will not be going alone."

The next few days were spent rearranging the boys' surgeries, ordering tickets, planning for the kids while Kevin and I traveled, speaking to Kelley's brother and sister, and checking on Peter. Everyone was so gracious and surprised that Kevin and I were traveling out there. They even offered to pay for our plane tickets, but a still small voice told me not to accept. Later, I would understand why.

Kevin and I arrived in Los Angeles, and Kelley's brother picked us up. He had agreed to host us during our stay. Kevin and I have always lived a very frugal life since we had been a one-income family for the last 19 years of homeschooling, and our vehicles were older than our teenagers. So, when Kelley's brother picked us up at the airport in a new Tesla, I had no idea how to even open the door to get in. I felt out of my comfort zone immediately. I would need to rely on God and Kevin to make it through my grief, the discomfort, and so much more.

Thankfully, Kelley's brother and his family were amazing hosts and incredibly hospitable despite their grief. Upon arriving at their home, I was introduced to Kelley's extended family members, including Kelley's mother. I had never spoken to her prior to this but had only heard about her from Kelley.

The second I saw her, my heart was reminded of the words God clearly spoke to me in January 2020, *"Everybody is somebody's child."*

I had initially signed up to donate for a mother, and here I was, hugging that mama whom I had prayed for the last three years. But instead of joyously hugging over a life saved as I had once envisioned, we were grieving together in each other's arms over a life lost.

"God, this isn't fair. No mother should have to bury her child," I inwardly told God.

God reminded me again of the pivotal fact that afternoon as I met Kelley's family, *"Everybody is somebody's child."*

What I had not initially realized was that this "donation story" was going to be so much bigger than just Kelley and her mother. The story was that everyone is a child of God. Peter, Morgan, and other family members came by to grieve together and to meet Kevin and me. God reminded me that each grieving relative was **His child** who was hurting, and He had sent me to give them hope. He had sent me to share His love with them. He had sent Kevin and me to that backyard in southern California to offer them peace.

The question "*Why?*" was asked of me a lot that day and the following days at Kelley's funeral and family gatherings. "*Why did I choose to donate? Why to a stranger? Why did we travel to California for the funeral? Why wouldn't we accept some funds to help with the travel costs? Why, why, why?*"

I prayed that my answers would be drenched in His Words. I recounted my 2020 pre-donation story to those who wanted to hear, my beautiful relationship with their beloved Kelley, and I spoke of the God who loved each one of them.

At Kelley's funeral, I was finally able to "meet" my dear friend in person. I sobbed and sobbed as I stared inside the open casket.

"*This was NOT how Kelley and I had planned to meet, God! She is in a coffin!*"

Thankfully, God values relationships and honesty, and I knew he appreciated me sharing my raw emotions with him. His answer was gentle and kind....

"***Share my love with her friends and family.***"

Kelley's family asked me if I would like to say a few words at the post-funeral lunch reception. I eagerly agreed. This would be my chance. God wanted me to donate to Kelley so that I could personally share my love with her. He was now bringing beauty from the ashes, wanting me to speak to her 200+ friends and family that afternoon so I could share His love with them.

I remember walking up to the microphone at the center of the reception hall. Some individuals, in the middle of the buffet line, stopped serving food onto their plates and stood still while I spoke. Others seemed to hold their forks midbite, pausing to hear my words. Before this moment, I had only been a name to these beloved friends and family of Kelley. Sure, the local paper in Charlotte published an article in December 2020 about my donation story, and I sent copies to Kelley, and she shared with the few that she would see in person during her personal recovery quarantine. But I was a stranger to all these grieving souls. They knew Kelley had received an organ from a stranger back east, but that was it. This was the first time most were seeing me or hearing my story. I asked Kevin to pray for me. I texted our kids back home to be praying, too, for this very moment.

Between the graveside burial and the drive to the reception hall, I only had time to quickly type a few notes on my phone. The planner in me wanted more time to write out what to say, but the Holy Spirit wanted me to rely on His Words rather than my own, and that is exactly what I did.

I recounted to them how my love for their beloved Kelley began in the "first trimester" seed-planting process, and how it grew for this stranger during the "second trimester" growth stage, and how eager anticipation nearly bubbled up from within me during the "final trimester." When I heard that Kelley had survived the transplant surgery and that my kidney was successfully filtering her blood, I told the crowd that it was like hearing, "Congratulations, it's a girl, and she has ten fingers and ten toes!"

Then, I was able to share with them a glimpse of the relationship and bond that Kelley and I formed and how we were blessed with two and a half beautiful years together. I learned to love Kelley for the feisty, funny female that God created her to be and whom they all had loved. And I told them how thankful I was that though I had given Kelley a kidney, she had given me a family in them.

I also jokingly told them that I felt compelled to share a few other things before the microphone was snatched away. I wanted to answer their inevitable question, "*Why did I donate to a complete stranger?"* As I have written in this book, I told them that it was because God cared about Kelley and every one of their relationships with Kelley. He loved them so much that He intervened in my life with what seemed like a crazy, radical idea to many. I shared with them a little about the character of God and how He is known for caring deeply and personally about individuals. He is also known for doing things His way, which is not always the way we would necessarily choose for ourselves. I reminded them that I would not have donated had he not instructed me to, and I had no doubt that everyone in that packed room would not have chosen it to be Kelley's time to leave this earth. But I encouraged them that we were to have faith because His ways are higher than ours. I also shared with them that my greatest pleasure was to share my faith with Kelley and how she had admittedly changed her view of God. I thanked them all for being so welcoming to Kevin and me while we were in California, and I reminded them that any friend of Kelley's was a forever friend of ours and that if they were ever on the East Coast, to reach out to us. I invited anyone wanting to come by and say hi to Kevin and me, for I wanted to hug them, for hugging them would be like me hugging a piece of Kelley.

I closed with **Numbers 6:24-26 NIV**. Knowing that there were those of Jewish and Catholic backgrounds in the room, I felt this would be a Scripture of blessing for all. I told them that for our first Christmas together, I had mailed Kelley a present that had daisies on it and that passage. We both shared a personal love of daisies, and every time she looked at that picture with the Numbers verse, I wanted her to remember that I was praying for her.

Looking around the room, I prayed that blessing over Kelley's grieving friends and family. *"May the Lord bless you and protect you. May the Lord smile on you and be gracious to you. May the Lord show you His favor and give you His peace. Amen."*

After I spoke, I sat down next to Kevin, who leaned over and encouraged me that I had done well. His strong, calm presence, along with the mighty strength of God, carried me through.

The rest of the reception was filled with hugging and meeting Kelley's beloveds, who were now like family to me. I met some who were devout followers of Christ who wore crosses around their necks and encouraged me in sharing my faith story, and others who simply wanted to thank me for giving them more time with Kelley.

Philippians 4 talks about a peace that passes all understanding which can only come from God the Father. I felt that peace so vividly during that trip to California. Yes, I sobbed and sobbed at the sight of my beloved friend lying in her coffin. But God gave me peace. That peace came in searching back through all our written communication. With the time difference and family and work schedules, Kelley and I would often have to settle for writing texts or emails to each other. At the time, this did not make us happy, for phone or FaceTime were always more pleasurable. But God. But God planned for my time of grief. I had countless messages between us. Those messages gave me peace as I could go back and read the progression of Kelley's faith during our two-and-a-half-year friendship. I saw how she went from asking me why to asking me to pray for her, to saying that she was praying to God for me, all the way to telling me she was thanking my Lord and Savior, Jesus, for our friendship. She had drawn close to God by having drawn close to one who knew Him and taught her about Him. **Philippians 4:7 MSG** talks about letting God know your concerns, and *"Before you know it, a sense of God's wholeness, everything coming together for good, will come and settle you down. It's wonderful what happens when Christ displaces worry at the center of your life."*

Points to Ponder

1. How do you handle plans that are beyond your control? Do you turn towards God and trust in His plan,
   or do you turn away from God during your pain and
   confusion? Do you need to turn back towards Him?

2. Read *Numbers 6:24-26*. Who could you pray this powerful
   prayer of blessing over today?

3. Read *Philippians 4:6-7*. What is causing you stress, worry,
   and anxiety in your life that you need to hand over to God
   right now? Let Him wash over you his perfect peace. Seriously,
   please do not turn the page until you have paused and handed
   over your concerns to the all-powerful Creator of the Universe
   who cares and wants to help you.

Devotion: Look Up

Written for a Community Bible Study Devotion, 2021

Colossians 3:2 NIV says, *"Set your minds on things above, not on earthly things."*

A few years back, I wrote a short story for my kids. It was titled "Mas." In case you aren't familiar with the Spanish language, "Mas" means "More." The story was centered around three kids, Anaile, Neb, and Mas. They had a few adventures, but their biggest challenge was that they were just never content with what they had or with life. And one day, through the help of a magical book that they found, they realized that they had been traveling in the wrong direction. Their new magical book acted as a compass and as a mirror. As a compass, they were able to begin walking forward instead of backward, and as a mirror, they discovered that they had even been seeing themselves backward. When they viewed themselves from the correct angle, they discovered their real names and identities. Anaile was really 'Eliana' spelled backwards. Neb was really 'Ben,' and Mas was actually 'Sam.' (These are the names of my three kids). I will come back to this thought in a minute.

Now, I want you to think about a map. When you plug an address into your GPS, you are given a dot on a map. My husband and I both have degrees in Geography and Cartography (map making), so we talk about maps all the time in our house. Now, if my iPhone gets lost, and I turn on the 'Where's my phone' app, I will only see a dot on a map, a two-dimensional picture. For instance, it may even be close enough to put that dot on my couch, on the southwestern wall of my living room. And I can tear all the cushions off and look under the couch and still not find my phone. Or another example could be if my cat got lost, and I checked online to see his microchip information. I could see where he went, and I might even know that he is in my backyard by seeing a dot in the corner of the map of my yard. If I walked outside and followed that dot to the corner of my yard, I still might not find my cat.

The problem with these scenarios is that a dot on a map is only contained in two dimensions. Think of a square, a simple four-sided polygon. However, if you added a THIRD dimension to a square, what do you get? A cube! In the example of my lost phone, I could not find it because it might not have been hidden under a couch cushion, it could be sitting on top of my bed, which is on the UPPER level of my house, directly ABOVE the living room couch. And in the example of my lost cat, he was not initially found because no one had bothered to look UP, for he might have been UP in the tree in the corner of my yard. The point I am trying to make is that a two-dimensional view of things will not actually help you see things clearly.

Ok, one last example. Have you ever been to a 3D movie? You are given special glasses to help you see the movie and fully experience it the way it was designed. And have you ever taken off those glasses to scratch your nose or to just peek at the screen without them? What you see is just blurry images. It makes no sense, for it is out of focus because you lose the third dimension and are stuck with an unclear two-dimensional view.

Now where am I getting with this - The story of Mas, the map, the movie? Well, the book of John is full of encounters Jesus had with people. And when Jesus spoke, they were often confused, not understanding what he meant. They were looking at what Jesus said through the simple lens of our two-dimensional physical world. Nicodemus could not fathom how one can re-enter their mother's womb to be born again. The Samaritan woman could not understand at first how Jesus' water would quench her thirst forever. And what about eating Jesus' flesh to forever take care of hunger??

But those who chose to have faith were given the Spirit's knowledge, and in a sense, they were also given the third dimension. It was like they were handed a pair of those 3D glasses to help make the images less blurry and instead to 'come alive.' They chose to look UP, to set their mind on things above, and were amazingly blessed by it.

How many times do you ask God for an answer to prayer, but you do not get the answer you want? Maybe you have been looking at things backward, like Mas in my story? Or maybe you have NOT been looking upward, like the example of the lost phone or cat. We must be praying continually for God to reveal to us His Spirit and to see things in the spiritual realm, the third dimension. Only then will we understand what it is to be born again, to drink the living water, to eat of the Bread of Heaven.

After my kidney surgery, my recovery was quite a physically painful experience. But when I only looked at the two-dimensional pain, I became overwhelmed. However, when I chose to put on my '3D glasses' and focus on what God was doing in both the physical and spiritual life of my recipient, I was able to handle the pain because I recognized that there was way more to that story than what I might have been feeling.

Our culture is very materialistic, but we are warned in Scripture to not conform to this world. **Romans 12:2 MSG** says,

"Don't become so well-adjusted to your culture that you fit into it without even thinking. Instead, fix your attention on God. You'll be changed from the inside out. Readily recognize what he wants from you, and quickly respond to it. Unlike the culture

around you, always dragging you down to its level of immaturity, God brings the best out of you, develops well-formed maturity in you."

What if we went about our lives in the world, but not really of it, but instead, with our 3D glasses on, setting our minds on things above? What if we did not worry about things - the decorated things, the wrapped things, the flashy things, the things we need to buy, order or ship. But instead, we focus our hearts on thanking Jesus for being willing to enter this harsh, two-dimensional physical world for us. For He did enter it, so that He could personally hand us each a pair of 3D glasses to finally be able to truly see who GOD is. And He promises to come again and personally escort us out of this physical, 2-dimensional world, and into Heaven. And guess what?? Heaven will be more like one of those four-dimensional movies at Disney or Universal Studios, where you not only wear 3D glasses but also feel the splashes of water, and you feel air blowing on you. Heaven will be the most amazing experience, and it will be for eternity!! So, do not let the troubles of this physical world steal your joy, but instead with the help of the Spirit, focus on the spiritual realm and prepare to be amazed. So, choose to look UP and set your mind on things above!

22

Final Thoughts

"It is good for me to be near you. I choose you as my protector, and I will tell about your wonderful deeds." Psalms 73:28 CEV

"Draw Me Close." Over the years, God has continually used this phrase in my life. It was the anthem He sang over me that day in graduate school when I realized I had desperately strayed far from Him. He asked if I was willing to let Him back into my life, and I knew I needed Him more than ever.

It then became my prayer, *"Draw Me Close to you, Father,"* as I earnestly sought His will over my life through the joyous blessings of childbirth, homeschooling, and mission work, but also through the deepest, darkest moments of loss and tragedy.

Additionally, it was my prayer, *"Lord, help me get to know my recipient. Draw Me Close to whoever receives my kidney."* And God heard that prayer and blessed Kelley and me with an instantaneous bond and friendship that only blossomed more beautifully every moment we spent communicating together.

In my love for Kelley, I prayed over her, *"Lord, help her to pray these words to you, 'Draw Me Close.'"* I desired for her to get to know me so I could show her the Father who sent me. I longed for her to seek a relationship with the One who loved her so much to direct me to an operating table as a radical measure for His love to be known.

Reader, I pray that my deepest thoughts and prayers have, in a sense, drawn you close to me. Though we may never meet in person, I sincerely pray that by obeying God, writing this book, and sharing my thoughts and experiences have given you a glimpse of who I am. And hopefully, just hopefully, when drawing close to me, you will ultimately see that it's not me whose story you are reading, but God's. I am not sure how you came across this book, whether you purchased it, were gifted a copy, or "randomly" found it somewhere. But I do not believe it was an accident. May you also pray, "*Draw Me Close.*" The Bible PROMISES that if you draw near to God, He will draw near to you. Whether you are far from Him, seeking the pleasures of this world to numb your aching soul because you do not know how else to soothe the pain, or if you are a believer in the Bible, we can all pray to draw closer to our Heavenly Father. He is standing there desiring a deep, beautiful relationship with you.

Time is a gift. Not until I donated my kidney had I really thought about having the ability to give that gift to anyone. God allowed my donation to give Kelley almost three additional years with her family. I thank you, reader, for the gift of your time and for reading these words I have written. That, too, is a sacrifice of its own. *James 4:14 NLT* reminds us of our brevity, *"How do you know what your life will be like tomorrow? Your life is like the morning fog—it's here a little while, then it's gone."* And *Ecclesiastes 9:12 NIV* states, *"Moreover, no one knows when their hour will come..."*

Time is a gift from God, and we cannot possibly know how many days we will be allowed to live on this earth. Eternity, however, is forever. God has promised his followers eternal peace in His presence. *Revelation 21:4 NIV* promises, *"He will wipe every tear from their eyes. There will be no more death' or mourning or crying or pain..."* I pray that you consider drawing near to God while you have the time.

God has a plan for everything. And I mean everything. As I look back over my life thus far, I see how God uniquely prepared me for the roles of student, wife, mother, teacher, missionary, runner, donor, and now writer. The path to preparation is not always easy, but God promises to use everything. *Romans 8:26-28 MSG* says....

> *"Meanwhile, the moment we get tired in the waiting, God's Spirit is right alongside helping us along. If we don't know how or what to pray, it doesn't matter. He does our praying in and for us, making prayer out of our wordless sighs, our aching groans. He knows us far better than we know ourselves, knows our pregnant condition, and keeps us present before God. That's why we can be so sure that every detail in our lives of love for God is worked into something good."*

As I mentioned in Kelley's chapter, she grew up with many health challenges, whereas I did not. However, the year following my donation surgery, I had numerous rare medical challenges. Most donors bounce back quite quickly from surgery, but that was not the case for me. Four weeks post-op, Kevin was taking me to the emergency room with severe abdominal pain, and no cause could be found. My incision never fully sealed, and I walked around with "goo" leaking from my abdomen for four months until my surgeon agreed to another surgery to seal it. So, Kevin drove me back to Emory in Atlanta in February 2021, and I underwent general anesthesia for a second time to have my incision sealed once again. For an entire year post-donation, I dealt with Small Intestinal Bacterial Overgrowth (SIBO), which is a rare complication of some abdominal surgeries. It seemed that whenever I ate, my stomach would bloat as if four months pregnant, causing me pain and discomfort, especially with all the internal healing that was trying to occur after having an organ removed. I became afraid to eat for a while for fear of the pain, and I lost weight I did not need to lose. I also developed an incisional hernia near the top of my incision at my belly button, and an old inguinal hernia from Ellie's pregnancy reappeared from all the internal shifting that had occurred. So, 364 days after my kidney donation, I was undergoing yet another surgery to repair both hernias at once. I went from never having stepped foot in an operating room to having three surgeries within a year. Even my closest prayer warriors were befuddled, wondering why God was allowing me to suffer when I had tried to be so radically obedient.

It took me a while, but I finally understood how that Romans verse above applied to my situation. I had prayed to God in 2020 to let me not only connect to my recipient but to show them how much God loved them. I tried hiding the initial health concerns from Kelley, but she was the type of person who you could not hide stuff from, especially with the close bond that we shared. I repeatedly told her that I was fine, that I wasn't concerned, and I never, ever, ever, ever regretted donating. I also told her how God must have had a plan for everything, that He had not failed me yet, and I would trust Him with my recovery. God showed me one day that He had allowed my medical trials that first postoperative year so that Kelley and I could relate better to one another. God was allowing me to enter her world. She had dealt with diabetic issue after issues her entire life. By God allowing me to suffer physically for a time, I could relate just a tiny fraction better to her scenario. And more importantly, she learned to relate to my spiritual perspective better. She repeatedly told me, *"I love seeing God through your eyes,"* for with every new challenge, I trusted God and His plan and shared that with her as well. If my medical challenges allowed Kelley to see God more clearly, then He was, in fact, answering my earlier prayers, focusing on the eternal rather than the temporal. Thankfully, God completely physically healed me. It took more time and challenges than I was expecting, but in the end, I would donate again if I had more spare kidneys.

Unfortunately, I do not have any more kidneys to share, but I do have my testimony. Two months after our surgeries, the Charlotte Observer published an article on my altruistic donation. I remember telling the reporter that I would only agree to the interview as long as my *"Jesus, Jesus, Jesus"* was not edited out of my quotes. I reminded him that there would have been no donation if Jesus hadn't directed me to donate, and there would be no article if Jesus wasn't allowed to be in it. In God's awesomeness, our story was on the front page of the Sunday paper, and everyone that weekend was able to hear about a God who cares about the intricate details in a person's life.

As a member of the Kidney Donor Athletes (KDA) group, I continue to run in races advocating for kidney donation and showing other runners that a person can still perform athletically with only one kidney. My hope is to help the thousands of others on the transplant waiting list possibly find their donor. More importantly, I never know when sharing my donation story might help me share God's love with someone who needs to hear it.

Through the National Kidney Donor Organization (NKDO), I had the privilege of mentoring numerous potential donors through the donation process. It was rewarding to be on the other side of the donation story, rallying others to their finish lines, supporting them, answering questions, and calming fears. Inevitably, everyone would always ask, *"So who did you donate to?"* Upon learning it was a stranger, natural curiosity almost always led to the next question, *"Why?"*

Smiling, I would happily share my reasons, for they all led back to Jesus and my faith in Him to always provide if I could simply trust and obey.

My heartfelt prayer is that you, too, saw God in my story,

page after page, while hearing my rawest emotions through the hardest and most joyous times in my life.

Over the course of reading this, I pray you have noticed God calling you to Him as well. Draw near to Him, friend. He wants to hear from you. He sent his son, Jesus, to something much worse than an operating table, to a tree on Calvary, so that He could show you His immeasurable love FOR YOU. He loves you that much! Receive that gift of love, and pray, *"Draw Me Close."*

Points to Ponder

1. Has reading this story piqued your interest in kidney donation? If so, please visit the National Kidney Registry or the National Kidney Donor Organization websites to learn more.

2. In *Ephesians 3:4-6 MSG*, Paul writes, *"As you read over what I have written to you, you'll be able to see for yourselves into the mystery of Christ..."* The Message is accessible and welcoming to everyone..." Do you believe that God's message is truly for everyone, including you?

3. Have you invited God to draw close to you? If not, what is holding you back?

4. The theme of God's ability to intervene in someone's life is all over this book. Looking back, do you see God's intervention in YOUR life? Seriously, please take some time to look back, pray, and contemplate this. Journal what you discover.

5. Do you have a testimony of God's love in your life that you can share with others so they can see God more clearly? If so, to whom is God telling you to share it with?

Devotion: Who Will You Meet?

Facebook, March 2017

Each day, ask God whom He would like you to MEET. We do this in our house, and it is neat talking about who God brings in front of you. And it instructs children (and adults, too!) to be looking around at others with Jesus-like eyes instead of constantly focusing on themselves.

So here it is...

M - Money. Is there someone who could use a little financial help? Maybe the lady in front of you in the grocery store doesn't have enough to pay for her groceries; maybe you want to pay for the people behind you in line; maybe you want to buy a homeless person a hot cup of coffee on a cold day....big or small, acts of generosity can be life-changing for both the giver and receiver.

E - Energy. Is there someone in your sphere of influence today who could use some of your energy? Go the extra mile to serve others, help someone whose arms are loaded down, open the door with a smile for the person entering behind you, and do a chore for someone in need.

E - Encouragement. Is there someone who is hurting? Do they need to hear positive messages of hope, love, faith, etc.? In America, we often try to put on a "happy, all is ok" face for others when we are really struggling internally. So sometimes, you might not initially notice those who need encouragement, but when guided by the Holy Spirit, you can be directed to just the right person with just the right words. Teach your kids to look for ways to show appreciation, gratitude, and kindness. (Often, if we follow a child's example, we can learn this from them!!)

T - Time. So often, we all have busy, busy schedules. We do not leave enough time to get everything done on our to-do lists, so we don't even think this is possible. The possibilities for this are endless, though!! Stop and pet the cat who is rubbing against your legs. Listen to the friend who is hurting and just needs to vent for five minutes or offer your shoulder for them to cry on. Maybe snuggle your kids an extra five minutes before bed tonight. They might need that extra snuggle time more than the five minutes of sleep. Let that car get in front of you - so what if you will get to your destination 6 seconds after them - your gift of generosity and time might be just what they need today.

So, who will YOU MEET today??

"Command them to do good, to be rich in good deeds, and to be generous and willing to share." 1 TIMOTHY 6:18 NIV

About the Author

Holly Armstrong - lover of Jesus, also claims the titles of wife, mother, educator, athlete, organ donor, missionary, author, and speaker, to name a few. She resides in South Carolina with her family and numerous fur babies. Holly holds a Bachelor of Science in Geography and Environmental Systems, a Minor in History, a Master of Arts in Education, and Post Baccalaureate Certificates in Instructional Design and Computer Based Training. She was a former computer trainer and training consultant but found her true passion in homeschooling her three children and teaching other homeschoolers in their homeschool cooperatives. In addition, Holly is a longtime member and leader at Community Bible Study (CBS) and is currently the Associate Teaching Director of her class in Charlotte, NC. Besides spending time with her family and cheering on her teenagers at their sporting events, Holly enjoys running, swimming, gardening, and taking prayer walks. Holly loves sharing her testimony of God's faithfulness to anyone who will listen, whether individually while in line at the grocery store or in a room full of people. Her heart is for her words and experiences to help others see God's faithfulness in their own lives and to draw closer to their Heavenly Father, who has a magnificent plan for their lives. She also prays that whoever hears the story of her kidney donation will also consider giving of themselves sacrificially, in whatever way God calls them.